CW01500106

Contents

Introduction

The Romans loved gardens. One end of a sarcophagus lid from Ostia Antica encapsulates the delight that they found in their beauty. A togate Roman relaxes in Elysium on a flowery bank shaded by trees. A mattock lies abandoned behind him while a basket of roses spills blossoms at his feet.

The earliest Roman town houses had little in the way of a hortus (garden) beyond perhaps a strip along the back of the property. Later some included kitchen gardens, but it was the development of peristyle gardens at the heart of the household and the social importance of owning a garden that spurred their development. Where space was lacking for a four-sided peristyle a trompe l'oeil painting provided one. Pompeii illustrates how houses were designed so that the garden might be glimpsed and impress from the front door. Greece had sacred groves but few domestic gardens to influence Rome. The pre-Roman Athenian house had mostly paved courtyards and, even after Augustan regeneration, Athens valued tradition and maintained the courtyard house rather than adopt the Italianate atrium home. Lack of water and rainfall was problematic for Athens until the Hadrianic aqueduct brought fountains into domestic courtyards, encouraging gardens. Less traditional Grecian cities such as Sparta, Patras and Corinth adopted Roman ways, developing their own versions of the atrium house. Atria were converted into peristyle gardens and became (as in the West) the focus of the house.

An agricultural people at heart, Rome's contact with the gardens of the Hellenistic East was to inspire them to develop an amazingly diverse and innovative domestic and public garden tradition. Aristocratic pleasure gardens (viridaria) encircled and dissected Rome, encompassing an eighth of it. Landscape and garden painting enhanced and influenced design. Their appreciation of natural beauty and landscape was probably unmatched until the eighteenth century. Just as modern gardens all differ, so, naturally, did those of the Roman world. Some were formal and geometric while others cultivated a wilder Arcadian appeal. They took delight in the juxtaposition of art and nature – the natural with the artificial – and in imposing decorative constraints on nature. Ivy could be trained into figural shapes or grown up columns and trees, while ivy mounds were formed around a stake. *Trompe l'oeil* paintings of plants and birds backed real flower beds. Topiary was popular and box, myrtle and bay were all used. Box was a popular edging for flower beds. Fishbourne gives a good indication of its possibilities, although one might question if this was what was actually planted there as the bedding trenches remained so intact. Just as Hellenistic architecture employed rhythmic alternation in pediment designs on façades, so great use was made of rhythmic or alternating curved and square niche shapes in garden pools, edgings and flower beds. Plantings were often architectural, fronting colonnades or water features like the Canopus at Tivoli. Imitating the convention of placing

ROMAN GARDENS

ANTHONY BEESON

AMBERLEY

For Susan Elizabeth Beeson, my sister-in-law.
Whose hanging baskets are the stuff of legend.

Acknowledgements

The author wishes to thanks, David Barnes, Andrew and Barbara Birley, Corinne Board, Richard Buckley, David Dawson, Robert Field, Nick Hodgson, Nich Hogben, Demetrios Michaelides, Marigold Norbye, David Neal, David O'Neill, Anastasia Panagiotopolou, David Reeves, Julia Sorrell and Mike Stone for their loan of images.

First published 2019

Amberley Publishing
The Hill, Stroud,
Gloucestershire, GL5 4EP

www.amberley-books.com

ISBN: 978 1 4456 9030 8 (print)
ISBN: 978 1 4456 9031 5 (ebook)

British Library Cataloguing in Publication Data.
A catalogue record for this book is available from the British Library.

Typeset in 9.5pt on 11pt Celeste.
Origination by Amberley Publishing.
Printed in the UK.

sculpture and urns in front of trees, so shrubs were planted before columns, as evidence from Oplontis shows. Planting pits and rooting pots (ollae perforatae) betray designs of lost gardens, even showing at the Spanish villa El Ruedo how trees were planted to shade the house. Recent studies at Stabiae's Villa Ariadne indicate with what care to gradient, drainage and irrigation some Roman gardens were laid out. The scientific study of Roman gardens is still a new one and owes much to the pioneering archaeological work of Wilhelmina Jashemski (1910–2007) in Pompeii and elsewhere.

Undoubtedly, fashion influenced garden design through the centuries, but its chronology is not well understood. The great age of garden sculpture seems to have been during the first century BC to the second century AD, with perhaps a partial revival in the fourth. In Britain findings at Littlecote, Latimer and Frocester suggest that random flower beds became the norm in later centuries, although centrally sited paths and pools such as at Spoonley Wood and Bancroft show a survival of formality also. Water played a huge part in garden design throughout the era and its presence had a significance that the modern world can hardly appreciate. Garden arts survived the fall of the Western Empire, kept alive in the east and by monasteries. Ideas were absorbed by Arabic invaders and in many respects Roman water gardens may be seen today at the Alhambra in Granada.

Rather than covering the botany of gardens, this volume is intended as a popular introduction to the decorative arts connected to Roman garden design, emphasising the great part that water played in that. It also covers the mythology associated with gardens. Especial attention is paid to the gardens on the Palatine and the exceptional ones of Conimbriga, Portugal.

Alan Sorrell's vision of an aristocratic garden in Rome (Courtesy and copyright of Julia Sorrell)

5

A Roman resting in the gardens of Elysium from a sarcophagus lid at Ostia.

First-century-AD garden design. Rhythmically niched box hedges at Fishbourne palace garden.

Chapter 1

A Garden Pantheon

Most Romans were deeply superstitious and religion permeated all aspects of daily life. Thus to understand Roman gardens, plants and their decoration it is necessary to first realise that they were full of religious allusions. Images of gods and heroes appeared not only for decoration but also for veneration although, unless found in a shrine or with an altar, it is not always easy to decide in what manner they presided.

Garden Shrines

Aediculae set into peristyle and garden walls combined the household gods with those of the garden. Paintings of agathodaemon serpents, bringers of prosperity and good fortune, together with their altars, decorated walls. Small temple-shrines on pedestals are found in Germanic provinces. Fine examples are in museums in Bonn and Luxembourg. Monolithic aediculae were popular such as the third-century-AD example from Quinta de Marim, Portugal, with its flanking

A third-century-AD monolithic garden shrine from the villa at Quinta de Marim, Portugal.

pilasters formed of sacred double Ss and lotus flowers. Full-scale built shrines also occur. Montmaurin in France featured a polygonal one while, in Britain, Chedworth and Darenth had them and Bancroft's octagonal building may have been one. A 1.98-square-metre foundation in the peristyle garden of House XIV.I at Silchester suggests an elaborately built structure with a stepped frontage. At Littlecote Roman Villa, Room 42, attached to the garden wall and directly opposite the southern entrance to the Orphic complex, may have been a shrine.

Venus

Venus, goddess of beauty and rebirth, patroness of gardeners and guardian of gardens, held the rose, lotus and myrtle as floral emblems. In her earliest Italic form she protected the vegetable garden, but later encompassed the flower garden. Her merging with the Greek Aphrodite, and her connection via Aeneas with the founding of Rome, saw her adoption as the mother of the Roman people. As Venus Fisica she was a universal creative force that stimulated the natural world. Sappho's invocation to Aphrodite (Fragment II) sang of her sacred temple amid an apple grove on Lesbos, of cool water and the ground covered with roses.

Roses were widely cultivated in the Mediterranean world. Paestum especially was famous for 'twice-flowering roses' and perfumes. Red roses were said to be infused with Venus' blood: bleeding from a rose-thorn prick, she stained white roses red for eternity. In art, Venus holds a rose or is surrounded by them. Her lotus symbolised regeneration, dying into the mud each winter and emerging in spring. Like her, it was emblematic of spring and its leaf, used as a fan, was held by her or accompanied her image. It suited the water-born goddess, of 'good sailing', and lotus flowers and buds often accompany Venus on mosaics. Myrtle was hers and was included in bridal flowers. The *Pervigilium Veneris*, that Roman paean to Venus and springtime, sings of her weaving myrtle bowers for lovers and sending her nymphs into myrtle groves. Myrtle appears in Pompeian paintings and was commonly encountered in gardens. Its aromatic, evergreen foliage lends itself to topiary and clipping.

Images of Venus appeared in Roman gardens. In Britain notable statues come from Ashwell and Dover. Popular depictions showed Venus kneeling, washing, putting on a sandal and drying her hair. They were suitable to place near water, as was the *Venus Callipyge*, depicting the goddess admiring the reflection of her buttocks. The *Venus Anadyomene* from Benghazi, Libya, in the Pennsylvania University Museum of Archaeology, depicts her rising from the sea and drying her hair. It was cut off at the thighs and was designed to be displayed on a submerged pedestal in a pool. In art, both the scallop and the dove represent her.

Venus was associated with nymphs and fountains. Hesiod derived Aphrodite's name from *aphrós* (ἀφρός) 'sea-foam', interpreting it as 'risen from the foam', which is highly appropriate when associated with fountains. A pose suitable for the nymphaeum is that of *Aphrodite of Perge*, where she holds a scallop shell before her. Cupid and dolphins act as her supporters in statuary, or as fountain spouts, as at Caerleon's nymphaeum. Her marine thiasus (retinue) includes tritons and nereids. Grand statuary groups depicting her triumphal natal voyage to Cyprus as depicted on mosaics must have existed in major pools. Two groups in the National Archaeological Museum, Naples, from the piscina of the villa at Formia depict nereids riding on pistrices, as does another from the villa of Pausilypon in the same collection. Garden paintings of Venus as a statue or divine living being were popular, although the setting might be marine rather than terrestrial. At the House of the Marine Venus (Pompeii), newly born, she reclines in a scallop shell. Mosaics of Venus adorn garden walls; most notably that depicting Neptune and Venus (protectress of sailors and maritime trade) overlooking the garden in the incorrectly named Herculanean House of Neptune and Amphitrite. A fragmentary mosaic displayed at the House of the Doli, Ostia, depicts her statue in a garden shrine with a garlanded altar flanked by candelabra.

Priapus

Priapus was the country god of fertility and gardens whose attributes were fruits, vegetables, flowers and a huge erect phallus. Rocket and mignonette were sacred to him. His painted portrait adorned the fauces at the Pompeian Houses of the Vettii and of Leda (discovered 2018). He protected against the evil eye, spells and sorcery, and his member was both apotropaic and also a threat to burglars. His worship originated in Asia Minor and spread to Italy via Greece. Generally considered to be Venus' son by either Bacchus or Mercury, he was cursed and malformed by Juno while in the womb. Priapus is often depicted as in a statue from Sousse, clothed in a long garment that he lifts, apron-like, to his chest to carry a bundle of fruit and vegetables while exposing a huge erect phallus. At Narbonne museum a heavily draped Priapus from Rocquefort-des-Corbiéres holds a basket of fruit accompanied by two amorini. The garment's frontal folds betray Priapus' aroused state beneath the fabric.

On a relief from Aquileia, Silenus leans across an altar to tie a sacred ribbon to the phallus of Priapus' statue. The phallus acted as a fountain spout on statues of Priapus from Aquilea and Pompeii's House of the Vettii. Small statues often wearing his Phrygian cap inhabited gardens and some see the Germanic gnome as his descendant, believing knowledge of him survived among country folk. A bronze Priapus from Rivery in the Museum of Picardy wears a 'cuculus', a Gallic coat with hood, and may have inhabited a garden shrine. It is in two parts, with the upper section being detachable like a candle snuffer and revealing a phallus on legs beneath. A pine statue of young Priapus from a Marseille shipwreck reminds one that sculpture could be in wood.

An impressive Priapus was discovered at Vindolanda Fort, Northumberland. It was recovered from the western rampart mound behind a large bread oven. Commenting on the discovery to the author, Vindolanda's Andrew Birley wrote: 'Of course the ramparts are well known to be places where gardening by the military took place so its location on them would be appropriate for such activities. Hadrian personally had a go at soldiers spending too much time on their gardening rather than soldiering so it is rather fun in that context.'

Bacchus

Ivy and grape vines were sacred to Bacchus, whom Greeks called Dionysos and the Romans merged with Liber, their god of fertility, viticulture and wine. The thyrsus, Bacchus' sacred staff, has various interpretations: sometimes ivy tops it and at others a pinecone. Alternatively it is a fennel stalk or the thick stem and head of an artichoke or related cardoon. As a rustic god and patron of the theatre, Bacchus' iconographical references are broad. His thiasus includes Ariadne, Silenus, Pan, centaurs, bacchantes, satyrs and fauns. Theatrical masks, drinking vessels, ivy, grapes and panthers were Bacchic symbols. Allied to his thiasus are Priapus, Silvanus, Sucellus and Hercules. Rurality, inebriated sexuality and enjoyment are imbued in his entourage, making Bacchic imagery popular in the garden. The twirling dance of the bacchantes and satyrs added a lively aesthetic to the generally static depictions of other characters. The torn animal parts carried by ecstatic bacchantes reminded of the cult's darker aspects, but he also promised resurrection. The god's pre-Christian ability to turn water into wine made his thiasus candidates for fountain sculpture. Silenus, his fat, balding companion, is a popular subject. Often intoxicated, satyrs support him or he reclines on an ass's back. Allied is Papposilenus, a hirsute, satyr-like aged representation of Silenus. Bronze thyrsoi formed standpipes in cantharus fountains and stylised marble copies ornamented gardens. Similar marble staffs supported heads of members of the thiasus, sometimes in janiform style.

Pan and Faunus

An Arcadian god of fields, woodlands and rusticity; of shepherds, flocks and rustic music. Pan was worshipped in natural places such as caves and grottoes. He was a deity of sex, fertility and springtime. Part goat and part human, his symbols were the pedum (shepherd's crook) and the syrinx (pan pipes). His sexual appetites made him an easy god to assimilate into the Bacchic thiasus and many a statue shows him aroused or attempting intercourse. Pan was an ideal subject for garden sculpture, especially where the garden was informal and Arcadian. Romans equated him with their ancient, horned, rustic deity Faunus (who remains obscure), but that the latter was still worshipped as a separate deity is proven by the many items dedicated to him in the fourth-century-AD Thetford Treasure. Visually and iconographically, it seems that Faunus and Pan appeared – and were – both one and the same to Romans. Both gods had affinities with Silvanus.

Silvanus

A god of woods and wild places, Silvanus protected plantations and flocks. He was also a god of boundaries, fields, fertility, farmers and the hunt. His worship did not raise large temples, but he was a god for the ordinary man. He is depicted with fruits and pinecones, the pine being sacred to him. He sometimes wears a wolfskin and often holds a falx (pruning knife) and a tree branch. He became equated with the Celtic Sucellus, who holds a mallet for striking boundary posts, often holds a pot and a syrinx or a sacrificial goat, and is also accompanied by a dog. Their iconography merged. Silvanus was popular throughout the empire. A fine statue base from a religious precinct at Keynsham and other altars together with reliefs from Chedworth and elsewhere prove his worship in Britain.

Cupid, Amorini and Putti

Cupid frequented Roman gardens. Otherwise known as Amor or, in Greece, Eros, his origins were debated. Some claimed that he was the earliest of the gods, but by the imperial age he was considered to be Venus' son by Hermes, Mars or Jupiter. Depicted as a beautiful, often rebellious, winged child or plump infant, he appears alone or as a supporter to Venus. Popular statues depicted the older Cupid stringing the bow that shot his feared arrows, or embracing the butterfly-winged Psyche. Examples of the latter subject are known from the Capitoline Museum, Ostia and Woodchester.

A host of winged infants, the amorini ('little loves') fill the archives of classical art. Generally male they are joined by psyches, again with butterfly rather than feathered wings. Amorini accompany many mythological characters. Popular as fountain and garden figures, with or without animals, and mimicking all aspects of adult life, amorini appear everywhere in Roman decorative art. They pose as the seasons or hold the torches of lust, life and death. The garden of Pompeii's House of the Vettii hosted several. Allied to the amorino and used in the same manner is the putto, the wingless non-human child.

Water Nymphs and River Deities

Attendant on Venus or Diana were the chaste water nymphs, deities of the bubbling spring or lazily flowing stream and eminently suited to grace the Roman garden as fountain sculptures. They are depicted as either standing, seated or reclining with an overturned jar from which water flowed, or holding a huge scallop shell before them. In the latter's original design the nymph was a secondary element of a fountain as the shell acted as a catchment for water spurting from a primary source that then overflowed into a pool. A mosaic of Diana bathing from Timgad (Algeria) depicts the nymph of the spring with a flowing jar while a waterfall fills her companion's scallop. A beautiful shell nymph in Istanbul Museum from a Romano-Cretan fountain includes a small drainage hole in the shell. Shell nymphs appear in painting and sculpture throughout the empire. A pair on pedestals flank the *Death of Actaeon* in a garden mural at Pompeii's House of Sallust. A superb, if damaged, second-century-AD shell nymph from Perge (Turkey) has been claimed as Aphrodite for its beauty, and occasionally the hairstyles mimic those of that goddess. Aphrodite/Venus is flanked by shell nymphs on the marine mosaic from Oudna (Tunisia). Occasionally shell nymph statues were bored for the insertion of a water pipe that spewed water into the shell directly. Examples survive widely from Saint-Romain-en Gal (there called Aphrodite) to Duntocher Fort, Dunbartonshire. A series of votive reliefs from Ischia, now at Naples, show three shell-bearers often accompanied by Apollo.

Other water nymph fountains survive in the corpus of garden sculptures including some charming seated examples. A delightful seated nymph fountain, based on the group *An Invitation to Dance* and depicted on a coin from Cyzicus, is in Naples Museum.

While nymphs encapsulate streams, the river deity is generally masculine and produced on a more massive scale to ornament public or aristocratic gardens. Usually reclining, the largest are accompanied by attributes that interpret their rivers to the viewer. Hence a sphinx and crocodiles will indicate the Nile or the wolf, and twins the Tibur. Cirencester's Corinium Museum holds the head of a possible river god.

Hercules

Hercules was welcome in the garden. Admired and enjoyed for his exploits and human frailties, he appealed to Roman society. Twice Hercules descended into Hades: to capture Cerberus and again to rescue Alcestis. His return was seen as a hope of rebirth and therefore he appears in funerary art. His labours, including the visit to the Garden of the Hesperides, link him to rurality. His drunkenness connected him to Bacchus, and he is depicted intoxicated or urinating as in the sculpture from Herculaneum's House of the Stags. Linked with Bacchus and Venus, he was worshiped as a protector of vineyards. In Italy his ancient connection with Ceres made him a symbol of fecundity. The white poplar was his tree.

The stylised Hercules' club was adapted for fountain standpipes and monoped table legs. Versions of the *Farnese Hercules*, showing the weary hero leaning on his club, were popular in the gardens of baths, gymnasia and houses. The Pompeian House of the Garden of Hercules had a huge garden that paleobotanical analysis showed grew aromatic plants, possibly used in the perfume or the medical trade. Its garden triclinium overlooked an altar and aedicula dedicated to Hercules.

The Muses, Pegasus and Apollo and Minerva

The nine Muses, daughters of Zeus and Mnemosyne, were patronesses of the arts, sciences and literature. From Mount Helicon, they promoted civic harmony and learning. Sculptural sets of Muses graced the grandest gardens and individual statues; such cycles are known from the Palatine and other Roman gardens, such as the Horti Variani. The Prado's eight-seated Muses came from Hadrian's South Theatre at Tivoli. Smaller gardens such as that of Pompeii's House of Loreius Tiburtinus have yielded examples. There, two Muses, both representing Polyhymnia, the muse of sacred poetry, dance and agriculture, survived on the otherwise empty row of bases overlooking the upper euripus. Her most iconic pose depicts her leaning on a pillar in contemplation. Some reliefs that may have been used as pinakes feature the Muses.

They were associated with water and especially Helicon's Hippocrene and Aganippe streams, struck by the hooves of Pegasus, and also the Peirene at Corinth. Pegasus' spring-making abilities made him a natural choice for fountain sculpture. Pausanius records Corinth's as depicting Bellerophon's capture of Pegasus, and water pouring from the steed's hoofs. Mosaics from Volubilis, Morocco, depict Diana bathing in a pool fed by water shooting from the mouth of a Pegasus fountain.

Apollo and Minerva appear in art with them. As their leader (Apollon Musegetes) Apollo's statue was found in the temenos of their cult centre at Helicon. A beauteous god, his full-sized image graced the grandest gardens, but Pompeii's yielded several bronzes. Bay and hyacinth were sacred to him; both commemorating unfortunates whom he had desired and were botanically immortalised. The aristocratic gardens of Rome held full-sized images and copies of famous sculptural cycles featuring Apollo, such as the flaying of Marsysas (found in the gardens of Maecenas and Lucullus) or the slaying of the Niobids as discovered in the gardens of Sallust and at Tivoli. Seven first-century-BC Niobid statues were discovered at the Ciampino villa of Marcus Valerius Messalla Corvinus in 2012–13. The over-life-sized statues once decorated the sides and central pedestal of a 20-metre pool into which they were toppled by an earthquake in the second century AD.

The olive grove was sacred to Minerva, but she rarely appears in garden sculpture beyond the grandest collections, sometimes depicted with Marsyas in copies of Myron's flute sculpture.

Diana

Mistress of the animals, and goddess of woodlands, the hunt and the moon. Often accompanied by her hounds or prey, Diana was an ancient Latin rural deity, principally worshiped in a grove at Aricia, near Lake Nemi, and was syncretised with the Greek Artemis, who shared many of her traits. Her huntress image fitted well into gardens that substituted for her natural groves. Allied to her are garden hunting sculptures found in gardens such as the boar and hounds from the House of the Citharist (Pompeii) or the deer savaged by dogs in the House of the Stags at Herculaneum. As protectress of the amphitheatre's venators her appearance alongside animals of the arena is explained. This encompasses those gardens where wild beasts sport on frescoes as if in a private nature reserve. A mosaic from El Jem depicts her in a nymphaeum surrounded by beasts. A garden fresco at Pompeii's House of Apollo depicted her statue in an ornamental pool. Sculptural cycles included her slaughter of the Niobids and the myth of Actaeon.

Flora and Pomona

Venus' prominence in the garden eclipsed Flora, goddess of flowers, and Pomona, protectress of orchards, who have left little trace among garden sculpture. A flower-crowned statue from the Pecile, Tivoli, called *Flora*, is in the Capitoline Museum, and two equally problematic examples are in the Farnese collection at Naples. Pomona, sometimes adapted from fountain images of standing shell nymphs (as in the Pompeian House of the Ephebe), is also represented by seated goddesses holding several apples at Cirencester and a shell full of apples from Alesia, France.

The Gratiae

Venus' thiasus included the Gratiae or Three Graces – Aglaea, Thalia and Euphrosyne – who may originally have been deities of vegetation. Roman art portrayed them naked, entwined and holding a rose, a die and a sprig of myrtle, as on the painting from Pompeii's House of T. Dentatus Panthera. The plants were emblems of their kinswoman Venus, while the die represented youth. Alternatively they hold roses as on the mosaic from Narlikuyu, Turkey, where they stand in a rose garden with a birdbath, doves and partridges, associates of Venus and emblems of love and fecundity. On Aphrodisias' Sebasteion one of the Graces holds corn ears, poppies and roses. They featured on a garden wall mosaic at Pompeii's House of Apollo.

CHAPTER 2

Front Gardens

The modern concept of front gardens, or gardens enhancing the exterior walls of a property, seemingly did not capture the Roman imagination. Town houses generally opened directly onto the street, but looked inwards. Even in the countryside, notwithstanding the desire for views, such gardens are a seeming rarity, although this conclusion may be through lack of investigation. In Britain the complex at Fishbourne was seemingly approached through a rather untidy assemblage of structures and was mostly inward looking. The great villa of Woodchester was also approached through what is considered to be a working courtyard. One true front garden may be found at the villa of Milreu in Portugal. There the main southern entrance was flanked by apsidal pools and the outside walls by long narrow gardens.

Garden Boundaries

Although stone walls often delineated and protected boundaries and gardens, other forms of security were regularly used. Excavations on waterlogged sites in London have uncovered evidence of the sort of wooden boundary fences encountered in Britannia and elsewhere at least in the first centuries of Romanitas. Early second-century-AD examples from the excavation at Poultry show that neat, thinly split oak pales were nailed to pole rails or base boards and then

A reconstruction of the remarkable first-century-AD spear-topped fencing found in London. (Author)

attached to posts driven into the ground in much the same way as modern panel fences are. More robust, wider and unevenly topped pales also survive, and some possibly derive from dismantled military palisades. Apparently, boundary fences were made high enough to ensure privacy and to provide windbreaks. By far the most surprising pales found at several locations in London have spear-shaped tops and must have provided an attractive boundary to a property or garden. Evidence for large native trees growing in back gardens was discovered. The Poultry excavation also provided evidence for a roadside box hedge dating from around AD 250–300.

Stone boundary fence posts with four slots cut into their narrow sides have been discovered at Villa Otrang, near Bitburg, Germany. Either individual planks or solid panels were slotted into these holes and posts are still in use on site. Wattle fences provided an additional, if less durable, way to delineate one's garden or property. Ditches might also be used to compartmentalise various divisions of a country estate.

Barren Courtyards?

Traditionally the pre-Roman Greek domestic courtyard was unplanted. At Fréjus, a mid-Augustan house in Formigé Square at first made do with a garden painted on the low walls and screen surrounding a herring-bone-paved peristyle with a puteal. In countries experiencing regular or heavy rainfall, peristyles lacking stone guttering and proper rainwater management may have been covered in gravel to ensure adequate drainage. However, excavated courtyards apparently covered in gravel or paving were not automatically devoid of plants. Apart from movable pots, urns and planters, 'keyhole' plantings of trees and shrubs that occur elsewhere in Roman courtyards are quite likely to have existed and to have been overlooked in excavation. House 3, Caerwent, and the commanding officer's house at Arbeia Fort are but two British examples where such plantings possibly occurred. The 1908 Villa Kerylos recreation of a Delian peristyle at Beaulieu-sur-Mer, France, aptly displays the possibilities of keyhole planting in an otherwise

The opus spicatum paved courtyard of an early Roman house in Frejus featured a painted trellis garden and a puteal above a cistern.

Keyhole planting and potted plants in the recreation of a Delian house's courtyard at the Villa Kerylos at Beaulieu-sur-Mer.

A rare 1903 excavation photograph of the Villa of the Aviary's garden at Carthage. The mosaic spandrels remarkably contained frames for living trees. (Author's collection)

paved courtyard. Apart from examples of keyhole planting recently recognised in Roman temple and public gardens, a surprising find in Carthage shows an example where trees were actually set into a mosaic. Surrounding the living octagonal garden of the Villa of the Aviary, each corner-filling mosaic panel, decorated with birds and animals and dotted with broken branches of shrubs and fruit trees, featured a small inserted stone frame into which trees or shrubs had been planted, thus juxtaposing the living with the imitation. The four trees must have mirrored in reality those mosaics where shading plants grow from each corner.

A Room With a View

Where possible, houses and reception rooms were placed so as to achieve the best views. Textual references and evidence from Campania show that glass screens and huge windows (sometimes with folding shutters) were employed in the first century. There is no reason to believe that these refinements were not available in later centuries and other provinces. Triclinia at Italica's House of the Birds and Utica's House of the Cascade were flanked by water gardens reminiscent of the Palatine's Cycizene triclinium where every diner was provided with a view. At Oplontis this idea was expanded so that reception room 69 in the east wing not only viewed the east and west gardens but its side windows opened onto light-well gardens in 68 and 70 and thence through other rooms' windows to internal gardens two chambers beyond those. From 65 it was possible to look through an enfilade of six chambers glimpsing three living gardens, reception rooms and walls covered with trompe l'oeil fountains and bushes. Light-well garden 87 was overlooked by a large bow-windowed chamber. Stabiae's San Marco villa also has a triangular light-well garden overlooked by a bow-window. Behind its colonnade the maritime villa at

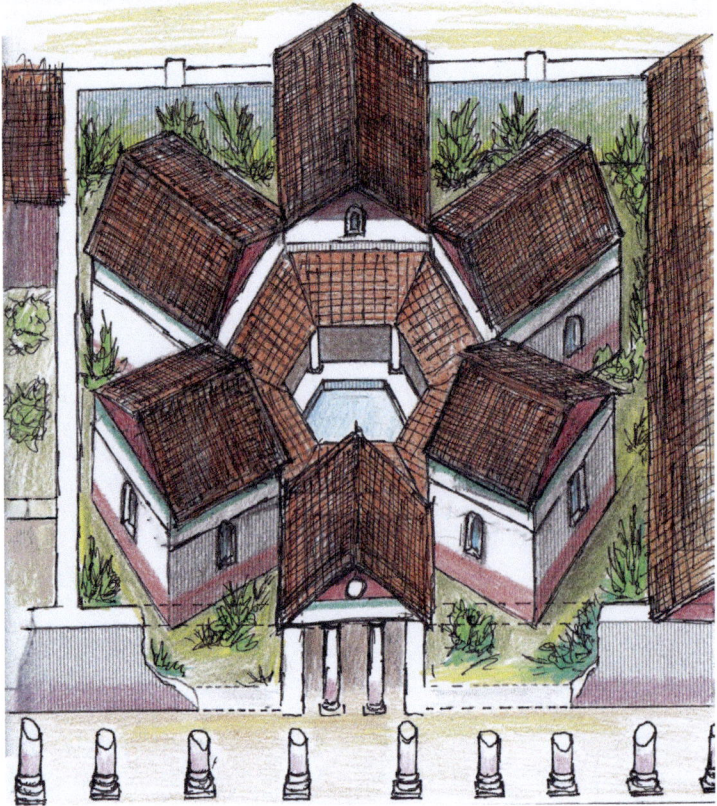

Abicada Villa, Portugal, showing the central internal garden court and its hexagon of chambers.

16

A view from Room 74 across a light-well garden through a reception room once panelled in precious woods to another garden and chambers beyond at Oplontis A.

Abicada (Portugal) was divided into three sections. Centrally a square, walled, garden court surrounded a complex of rooms grouped around a hexagonal peristyle and pool. Adjoining this section was a reversed peristyle garden. Its colonnaded ambulatory surrounded a central chamber that viewed flanking side gardens.

Planters

Roman gardens made great use of raised flower beds or planters. They ranged from large troughs to long raised beds and narrow wall-top channels, and presented novel ideas for floral display. For those relaxing in rooms opening on to peristyles they would have provided a highly visible border of living colour. They were also a sensible solution for light wells, atria and small peristyles, especially in areas lacking good soil or a plentiful water supply. In Campanian gardens one finds them used in delightful ways. In the House of the Mosaic Atrium at Herculaneum, the peristyle wall holding the large glass and timber screens included a gutter-like window box channel. In the House of the Alcove 'window boxes' were formed in the window-like openings formed by the piers of the little peristyle. Again, at Herculaneum they line the sides of the atrium's impluvium in the House of the Relief of Telephus. The peristyle of the House of the Lovers at Pompeii was surrounded by a high gutter planter, while at Oplontis the light-well pool and fountain of Room 16 itself featured a circular planter for water plants. In North African cities where rainfall was problematic, peristyle or atrium gardens were the norm by the third century AD. They were a useful way of bringing refreshing greenery into the home. The peristyle of Timgad's House of the Planters was lined with an undulating bow-fronted planter featuring a series of four bows on each side. At the House of 'Omnia tibi Felicia'

Oplontis A: the light-well fountain and circular planter in Room 16. The pool was painted blue for added effect.

The House of the Planters at Timgad, Algeria. (Author's Collection)

(May everything bring you happiness), Dougga, Tunisia, a series of planters surround a small impluvium court paved with a zig-zag 'water' mosaic, indicating its underlying cistern. Planters surround the rhythmically niched pool beside the triclinium in Conimbriga's House of Cantaber and would have added to the beauty of the scene. La Cocosa Villa, Spain, had a raised shallow trough surrounding the paved peristyle as a podium for pot plants.

Hanging and Sunken Gardens

Roman garden designers took advantage of the opportunities afforded by the architecture and settings of buildings. Level surfaces were desired on which to construct buildings and so hillsides were terraced and extended outward by vaulted platforms on which to build chambers and porticoes. Maritime villas are depicted as founded on arcaded platforms, sometimes used as boat sheds, and at Fréjus the modern name of La Plate-Forme given to a maritime villa enshrines this. The Stabian Villa Ariadne had castellated terraces and ramps facing and descending to the sea. The great villa at Sirmione overlooking Lake Garda is surrounded by a vast arcaded platform and equipped with cryptopotici, those cool semi-basement corridors, so useful for storing perishables, facilitating staff movement and escaping the heat of high summer. By early imperial times their use was widespread and they occur at the Palatine, Castel Gandolfo and Tivoli. The decorative possibilities of hanging gardens was soon realised and the gardens of Tiberius' Palatine palace flourished on vaulted chambers covered with imported earth and capable of bearing trees. Pompeii's Villa of the Mysteries has two L-shaped rose gardens above cryptoportici and the House of Fabius Rufus on the city wall had gardens on three levels, including a hanging garden with a fountain pool. The bow-fronted façade of the house overlooking this terrace is somewhat reminiscent of the wing recently identified

The sunken garden of the House of the Anchor Pompeii. (Author's Collection)

The Villa of Diomedes, Pompeii, in the 1880s with an early attempt to restore the original planting scheme. Carbonised trees were discovered during excavation. (Author's Collection)

overlooking the Palatine's hanging water garden. Also on the Palatine a vast Flavian hanging garden arose on vaults overlooking the Colosseum. Mausolea like those of Augustus and Hadrian also supported vast hanging gardens planted with evergreens symbolic of immortality.

Sunken gardens were also a Roman speciality. Peristyles were often around 20 cm higher than their gardens to prevent rainwater and mud from dirtying the floors. At Herodium, Herod's peristyle was 1 metre above the landscape garden, presumably to afford better views across to its pool. Of dramatically sunken gardens, probably the Stadium and Sunken Peristyle on the Palatine are the best known, but Pompeii's House of the Anchor displays an elegant example reached by a ramp from the ground floor. The garden was bordered by rows of arched niches holding pedestals intended for statues or flower baskets. Two wide round-headed niches flanked a pedimented aedicula at the southern end and held fountain figures. Alternating columns and piers lined the gallery above the garden. The House of Apollo's sunken garden had a deep circular pool painted blue, a cascade and numerous small sculptural pieces. It was surrounded on three sides by a terrace wall painted with plants and birds. Pompeii's Villa of Diomedes' vast enclosed garden was viewed from the house above and arcaded ambulatories terminating in belvederes. A columned pergola overlooked its central, rhythmically niched, pool. Carbonised trees suggest plantings in beds either side of the garden. The photograph of 1880 shows an early replanting. Herculaneum's House of the Hotel's orchard garden lay 1.10 metres below its surrounding peristyle.

Herod employed Roman designers for his third palace at Jericho. They created a spectacularly framed 145 by 40 metres sunken garden backed by a high and elaborate rhythmically niched terrace wall with a central theatre-like cavea of planting terraces. A wide water channel fronted this façade. Colonnades 2 metres above the garden provided viewing platforms at either end. Elements remind one of Conimbriga's Trajanic bath's sunken garden.

Narrow sunken gardens flanked the Cycizene triclinium at Stabiae's Villa Ariadne so that the tops of flowering shrubs were seen by diners through its vast windows. Topography also provided the chance to design sunken gardens to be viewed from above such as at Vaison-la-Romaine's House of the Arbour or Dougga's Trifolium House. In Tunisia's Bulla Regia, basement garden courts offered escape from the summer heat.

Trellises, Pergolas, Fences

Roman murals show the importance of trelliswork in garden design. It provided the practicalities of division and plant support, but also the aesthetic contrast of formality against nature's informality. Few examples of wooden trelliswork survive, but its portrayal in art, and exact imitation in stone, allows one to understand its construction.

In its simplest form canes of willow or dogwood were arranged diagonally and woven and tied together at each crossing. Soil impressions from a very light trellis that was little more than reeds or canes have been noted at Pompeii's House of the Painter and recently restored at Oplontis. More substantial wickerwork was used for the elaborate and closely woven trelliswork panels forming arbours and topped by basketwork jugs and urns that appear in mural painting. The dining arbour on the Palestrina Nilotic mosaic is woven. Different coloured cane was used in panels for contrast, as appears on the murals of Pompeii's House of the Orchard.

Diamond lattice trellising of flat lathes was joined at the crossings by bolts with circular metal washers. Marble copies used as transenne at villas like Rabacal (Portugal) and at Leptis Magna's nymphaeum reproduce this. Even the fourth-century mural of a wilderness garden restrained by trellising in the southern Theoderican hall at Aquilea shows these washers. Long

Restored lightweight trelliswork at Oplontis A. Casts of the original tree roots scatter the grass. The east wing with the door to reception Room 69 and the swimming pool is far left, beyond.

A nineteenth-century engraving of a trellis painting from Herculaneum with woven arbours and vases. (Author's collection)

A copy in stone of wooden trelliswork from the Nymphaeum at Leptis Magna, Libya.

rectangular panels of cross trellising were strengthened by the inclusion of centrally placed and more substantial uprights forming square lattice trellis (again as at Leptis), but occasionally the narrow cross-trellising formed a backing to rectangular panels of square lattice, with the larger wooden elements supported at intervals by substantial upright fixing posts. In these cases the size of the joint washers is increased to reflect the larger struts. This is shown clearly on a stone panel from a house just south of the House of the Cascades at Utica (Tunisia). Large-scale wooden trellis, employing both diamond and square lattice of equal size to form panels, was also commonly employed and appears on murals. Trelliswork would incorporate panels of differing design for variety, as seen on the garden murals of Pompeii's House of the Great Fountain. Practical fencing and pergolas joined the purely decorative in gardens. Mosaics

Right: A photograph from around 1890 of the restored garden at the House of the Centenary with the pergola over the fishpond. (Author's collection)

Below: The preserved section of carbonised wood and glass screening along the garden corridor of the House of the Mosaic Atrium, Herculaneum. The wall top included a window box.

depicting nymphs watering and harvesting roses from Sidi-Ghrib (Tunisia) display an unusual border fencing of close-set palings bound by rope at the base, centre and top. The cemetery garden mural at Sidret-el-Balik, Libya, depicts amorini threading grapevines onto a large trellis. Another scene depicts a villa courtyard covered by diagonal vine trellis. Garden triclinia and fishponds were shaded by pergolas and vines.

A dwarf wall or pluteus that might be painted with plants as a trompe l'oeil extension to the living garden often surrounded the peristyle garden. Alternatively, slots in columns show that wooden or stone trellising was fixed between them. Pierced stone transenne panels from intercolumniation survive from Rabacal. Slots below a capital and on the stylobate at House 3, Caerwent, suggest that the intercolumniation was partially filled by a high trellis although, at Pompeii's House of the Ephebe, similar holes suggested to its excavator, Maiuri, that the peristyle was partially enclosed by a wooden and glass screen to shield rooms from inclement weather. Most columns of its lower peristyle also were linked by a wooden bar at a height of 1.70 metres that Mauiri believed was hung with curtains. Pliny's D-shaped peristyle at Laurentum was fully glazed, probably like that at Herculaneum's House of the Mosaic Atrium.

Both wooden and stone trellis could be used to effect in the same garden as is seen in the paintings of the Garden Room of Livia's villa from Prima Porta. There a wickerwork trellis fronts a lawn leading to a white stone trellis featuring alcoves for specimen trees and composed of panels of three designs. A wilderness of fruit trees and shrubs burgeons behind. Stone trellising not only fossilises the designs of wooden ones but also includes non-timber designs. The imbricated scale design possibly arose from grills or open panels being constructed using imbrex roofing tiles. An unusual panel of intersecting circles survives from the temple at Milreu in Portugal. In England, Great Witcombe, Chedworth and a putative temple in Cirencester have all produced examples of large stone panels based on a confronted S design. Erroneously called balustrades, these are actually uniquely large-scale roof ornaments and used either as individual acroteria or, in the case of one of the curved Chedworth examples, as a running cresting on the nymphaeum apse.

Close-set palings and a nymph watering roses from Sidi-Ghrib.

CHAPTER 3

Statuary and Garden Ornamentation

Unless discovered in situ it is impossible to determine whether sculpture was intended for the house or garden and, even then, one can only say that it was discovered at its final resting place. The peristyle garden was the prime location for displaying sculpture and much of what is now in museums will have come from such an environment. Care was taken to provide reception rooms with the best view of a collection. Life-sized or larger human statuary is rarely encountered in the average domestic garden. These appear in imperial, aristocratic, public or religious contexts. The great age of garden statuary and ornaments dates from the first century BC to the second century AD. The phenomenon seems to be most prevalent in Italy, and centred on Rome, but those elsewhere wishing to display their Romanitas and wealth followed the fashion. The lack of sculpture at Fishbourne, Southwick and other early British villas is surprising but probably it was recycled later. There was a thriving business in copies and interpretations of famous sculptures to add to genuine antiques. Some collections were

The design of the first-century-AD villa at Southwick, Sussex, was greatly influenced by that of Fishbourne and probably had the same architect. (Author)

25

vast. Pliny, writing to Rufinus (Letters 92), mentions Tullus' collection of 'curiosities' that were to be auctioned: 'He had such an abundant collection of very old statues that he actually filled an extensive garden with them, the very same day he purchased it.' Some sculpture was legally seen as fitments and houses were purchased for their collections. Large-scale sculpture display was treated architecturally so that a row of statues acted as a visual colonnade. Statues and urns were placed before trees or columns or spaced between colonnades. The shimmering reflection of water was believed to bring a statue to life in the viewer's mind.

The majority of sculpture used in middle-class gardens was locally made and, unless of bronze, reliant on suitable stone being available. Oscilla, herms, children (playing, sleeping and with animals), and Bacchic subjects were most popular. Other genre subjects especially suited to Arcadian gardens included fishermen and shepherds. Athletes and wrestlers graced grand gardens. Sculptures of wild and domestic animals are often found. Everything from snakes to hounds occur – sometimes adapted as fountain sculpture.

Possibly in the provinces, formality in garden design began to go out of fashion in the second century AD and more natural effects cultivated. At Chedworth the central courtyard appears to have been laid to grass, but with scattered trees, shrubs, water features and the occasional garden ornament. A boundary or terrace wall behind the north range possibly supported additional gardens beyond. At the late Roman villa at Rabacal (Portugal) the octagonal central garden had outcrops of natural rock so perhaps trees and shrubs created an Arcadian landscape surrounded by the balustraded portico. However, fourth-century caches of garden sculptures from the villas of Quinta da Longas (Portugal), Valdetorres (Spain) and Woodchester, together with the herms of Welschbillig, may suggest an 'antik' revival. The formal trellises and balustrades that still appear in fourth-century garden murals, such as in the southern Theodorian aula at Aquileia, testify to the longevity of earlier ideals. Villa owners in the Iberian Peninsula are believed to have been importing garden sculptures from Aphrodisias and the eastern Mediterranean as a status symbol as late as the fifth century AD.

Birdbaths

Artistic representations prove that Romans delighted in the presence of birds in their gardens. They added movement, song, beauty and sentiment. The *Doves Mosaic* from Tivoli (now in the Capitoline Museum, Rome) is the most famous representation of birds drinking from a bowl, but this is a common theme in Roman art. Birds are shown drinking from fountains and basins that have little practical purpose other than to have been designed

Garden sculpture and basins at the House of the Vettii in the 1930s. Early photographs are most useful for documenting items now confined for safety to museum stores. (Author's collection)

26

The Three Graces in a rose garden mosaic from Narlıkuyu, Turkey, features a labella-type birdbath.

for their benefit. Drinking appears to be the limits of their artistic activities, but no doubt Roman birds also bathed. Apart from circular birdbaths (resembling the labella of Bona Dea rituals), there are shallow rectangular basins on stands that are a common feature of Roman gardens. Sometimes these are receptacles for fountain jets, but often they stand alone as hand-filled basins and are presumably also bird baths. Pompeii's House of the Vettii has examples, but fragments survive in Britain at Chedworth, North Leigh and an elaborately decorated piece comes from South Farm Villa, Draycot Foliat. Shallow semicircular basins, perhaps once mounted on pedestals, widely survive from Zeugma in Turkey, to Fishbourne and Verulamium in Britain.

Garden Furniture

Pliny writes of marble garden chairs while stone monopodium tables survive, but other wooden or bronze furnishings must have found a place outside. Carthage's *Dominus Julius* mosaic (now in the Bardo) features a garden scene with a bench, a wicker chair and the dominus on an upright chair with a footstool. A curved masonry garden seat attached to a screen wall survives at House 1, Empúries. Alfresco dining was popular and permanent masonry garden triclinia (and biclinia), once covered with thick mattresses, survive. These were shaded by vine-clad pergolas – often wooden, but sometimes supported on columns, as at Pompeii's Villa of Diomedes. They were the outdoor equivalent of the Cyzicene triclinium whose windows afforded views on all sides. Garden triclinia often had attached nymphaea as at the House of the Columns at Saint-Romain-en-Gal, providing fountain spouts (sometimes from the couches themselves), and pools to cool and delight diners. A table was founded in a central pool and dishes could be floated before guests as an extra conceit. The Nilotic Palestrina mosaic depicts revellers in a woven vine-clad bower through which the waters flow – possibly the ideal that

Romans attempted to emulate. Britain has, so far, not produced masonry garden triclinia, and most likely wooden furniture was used when required.

Depictions of hunting parties show the use of curved portable mattresses called stibadia for alfresco dining. These gradually became the fashionable shape for dining and the stibadium couch predominated in later Roman dining rooms and gardens. Masonry examples survive along with serving tables in the funerary garden of Sidret-el-Balik, Libya. One survives (with waterworks) at Almedinilla villa, Spain, and a great stibadium curved inside Hadrian's Serapeum at Tivoli.

Garden Urns

Plants had been grown in containers since earliest times and Roman mosaics and murals are full of representations of cantharus-cum-crater-style garden urns of various styles and elaboration. Mosaics suggest that they could be of bronze as well as marble. Reused amphora are also depicted. The use of all of these Bacchic-inspired vessels for ivy and vines was particularly pertinent. 'Obelisks' of clipped bay laurel were a favourite for cantharus urns, but other shrubs and flowers would have grown equally well. As today, any domestic vessel could be adapted for use, as seen on the Daphne Adonia mosaic, where a jug and a small amphora serve. Garden urns might stand in the rhythmic alcoves formed by hedges or trellising or interposed with plantings. A symbolic garden mosaic from Loupian villa (France) shows them placed between the columns of a peristyle. Occasionally, woven baskets were used to grow flowers in or to act

A restoration of one of a pair of unusual urns discovered at Chedworth stone store by the author during the preparation of this volume. (Author)

as a cachepot. Aristocratic gardens sometimes featured huge garden urns. Several found on the Mahdia wreck are now in the Bardo. Sometimes shapes were unconventional. The author recently discovered two fragmentary square-topped containers resembling reversed column bases (but unmatched on site) with plinth and a reduced torus ring in Chedworth's stone store (Inv. 73315.1/2).

Garlands

Festive and religious occasions saw the peristyle decorated with garlands (corona longa) hung between the columns and oscilla or draped over sculpture and shrines. Ancestral busts and diners were decorated with chaplets of sweet-smelling plants. A delightful mosaic from Carthage depicts putti decorating a tholos with rose garlands. A mural in the Palatine's House of Livia depicts beribboned garlands hung with wicker versions of sacred objects, such as the Bacchic liknon and Apollo's kithara. Where large enough, gardens provided the materials such as ivy, evergreens and flowers, but alternatively professional garland weavers connected to large commercial gardens were at hand. Depictions abound of the gathering of flowers and weaving of garlands. Strings or trailing plants were attached to a hook and then plaited, incorporating blooms and foliage as work progressed. Roses were especially favoured and depicted in African provinces and a mosaic from Thuburbo Maius consists solely of rose-petal garlands, birds and roses.

Dancing putti wearing the corona convivialis (rose chaplets) garland a tholos. Roses cover the ground. A mosaic from the Antonine Baths at Carthage.

Herms

Herms enjoyed a long popularity. The Greeks believed them to be apotropaic. They ornamented crossroads and boundaries but also protected buildings. Mostly stone but sometimes bronze, in Roman gardens their function was mainly decorative and their subjects often included members of the Bacchic thiasus. Originally four sided and topped with a bearded head of Hermes, to whom the number four was sacred, they often sported genitalia, as he was originally a phallic, fertility deity. Gradually they came to be topped by the heads of other deities and mythological figures, especially those connected with Bacchus. Roman herms might feature busts of statesmen or literary figures. Some had shoulder cross-beams on which garlands and cloaks were hung. Janiform or two-headed herms became popular decorative items.

Female herms are rarer and often archaistic. Examples come from the Palatine and gardens of Maecenas, Rome and also from House 2 at Empúries, Spain. Bacchantes and Ariadne feature among the subjects chosen.

The heads can sit upon carved marble pillar stands and be made of different materials to their supports. When several were used in a garden their upstanding eye-catching appearance could enhance the outline of flower beds as occurs in Pompeii's House of the Golden/Gilded Cupids, and increase the perspective effect of a garden when seen from the most important viewpoint

The garden of M. Lucretius, like a stage, formed the back wall of the house's tablinum. This 1870s photograph shows its original Bacchic sculptures. (Author's collection)

30

Some of the fourth-century herms from the great pool at Welschbillig, as displayed at the Rheinische Landesmuseum, Trier. The transenne have been restored as panels of imbrication.

as occurs in the garden of the House of M. Lucretius. A mural in the House of the Wedding of Alexander shows painted herms supporting pinakes. Herms also served as uprights between transenne to form barriers, as appears in the depiction of the imperial box on the obelisk base of Constantinople's hippodrome. When used thus the heads became finials, while their supports were given side grooves into which the panels slotted. The finest collection of herms used in this manner bordered a 58.3 by 17.8 metre pool at the palatial villa of Welschbillig near Trier. Constructed around AD 370, originally 112 herms are believed to have been used and seventy-one are now in the Rheinisches Landesmuseum, Trier. They portray emperors, philosophers, ethnic and mythological subjects and are remarkable for being a complete collection produced for a contemporary scheme at a time when sculptural decoration of gardens seems to have gone into decline. The pool itself echoed a hippodrome with a spina sporting fountains, so the surrounding herms and transenne in themselves reflected actual circus fitments. A fine bronze herm railing with janiform heads and horizontal rails was found in the second imperial vessel retrieved from Lake Nemi. In Cologne's Römisch-Germanische Museum a mausoleum relief depicts trellis panels separated by calyxes with human forms growing out of them to form herms.

Lampadophores

At Pompeii provision for outside evening enjoyment was made with hanging lamps (lychni) or wall brackets to hold oil lamps. Marble candelabra were among the cargo of the Mahdia wreck and furnished aristocratic gardens. The famous bronze ephebe (youth) from the House of the Ephebe had been transformed into a lampadophore to hold two candelabra branches for garden use. Other beautiful lampadophores ephebi come from Antequeras and Volubilis. The bronze Cupid found in Cirencester in 1732 also seems to have been a lampadophore. Those figures holding trays, often considered as serving tables, would also have held oil lamps both in the house and garden. Tarragona archaeological museum has a bronze African boy holding a tray on which is inscribed 'lucerna' (oil lamp).

Oscilla

The oscillum (plural oscilla) was suspended from trees and between the columns of a portico or an arbour's frame where they oscillated in the wind providing interest in their gentle movements and defending against the evil eye. Generally of painted marble or terracotta, although also produced in wood and metal, the majority date from the first century BC to the second century AD.

Oscilla, herms, sundials and pinakes as once displayed in the garden of Pompeii's House of the Golden Cupids. (Author's collection)

A pelta oscillum with gryphon terminals from Cordoba in the Cordoba Archaeological Museum.

The *Rape of Ganymede* oscillum as previously displayed in the Venice archaeological museum.

Their origins possibly lay in the Greek practice of displaying captured enemy shields, but they were also connected to the cult of Dionysos/Bacchus and their decoration often featured members of his retinue. Oscilla were suspended by chains, wires or ribbons. The basic oscillum was circular and carved on both sides. Satyrs and mythological characters, theatrical masks, dancers, actors and animals were common subjects. The pelta oscillum was crescent-shaped like an Amazon's shield and with confronted gryphon-headed terminals. Such peltae appear on distance slabs on the Antonine Wall. A relief from Vaison-la-Romaine depicts what may be a bronze pelta oscillum, complete with the Amazons' crossed axes. Rectangular oscilla existed and damaged examples are in the Vaison collection. Their decoration includes hares and rabbits eating grapes, Priapus, Pan and masks. Unusual oscilla at Vaison include small marble palmettes and a three-quarter round female head with a fish decoration on the reverse. Occasionally heavy double-sided reliefs depicting oscilla and their ribbons topped walls and pedestals. One depicting a satyr and Medusa oscillum was found at Quai des Etroits, Lyons in 1811.

The theatrical mask was one of the most popular oscilla and possibly many of the broken terracotta masks found in Northern Provinces were originally used as such. An unusual variant of this type was to carve the actor's mouth within that of the mask. Such an example came from the portico of La Estación villa at Malaga. Masks of Pan and Silenus add to the repertory. Oscilla were not confined to gardens but also ornamented theatres. Horizontally suspended marble oscilla lamps with bosses featuring Medusa or masks, and up to eight branches, joined normal oscilla in grand porticoes and theatres. The masks and peltae designs also featured in mausolea decoration. Occasionally hanging three-dimensional 'flying' sculptures were used in the grandest of porticoes. The famous marble *Rape of Ganymede* after Leochares, now suspended in the Tribuna of the Palazzo Grimani, Venice, and possibly looted from Constantinople, was probably such an example. Bronze hanging sculptures of a dancer and Cupid lyre player were among the Mahdia shipwreck cargo now in the Bardo, Tunisia.

Pinakes

Allied to oscilla were pinakes (singular pinax), carved and polychromed rectangular plaques that were mounted on pillar stands or attached to trellis posts in the garden. Pompeii's House of the Golden Cupids had many, both in the garden and built into its peristyle wall. Occasionally they decorated wall tops. The fresco in Room 8 of the House of the Orchard in Pompeii apes the interior of a lightly built, trellis-bordered wooden dining pavilion. Painted marble pinakes on stands appear amid the thickly planted garden, but the white pavilion supports several more Egyptian styled examples. Given the flimsy nature of the structure these must represent true panel paintings rather than marble pinakes. Damaged oscilla could often end their days adapted as pinakes.

Pinakes on stands, a herm and a mask and circular Oscillum in the House of the Golden Cupids. (Author's collection)

Putealia

The puteal (wellhead) was ubiquitous in the classical Mediterranean peristyle. Putealia protected stored water and facilitated drawing it in buckets from the rainwater cistern below a courtyard or garden. Their rims often display the marks of ropes. Whereas the water received into an atrium's impluvium cistern and used for consumption was filtered, that deposited in a peristyle's gutter and from thence into another cistern, was not. It was used for watering plants during high summer when rainfall might be unreliable. Every garden and courtyard in Pompeii is believed to be provided with its own cistern. Roman putealia can be plain or sculptural, ranging from simple fluting to mythological scenes. They were generally sealed with stone lids to protect water from dirt and sunlight.

Sundials

The Horae, or hours of the day, were associated with Venus and so, as patroness of the garden, sundials had their place in her domain. Sundials might be placed among the other garden statuary as in the House of the Golden Cupids at Pompeii or mounted at the edge of a pool or on its central island as at the House of the Cascade at Utica, Tunisia. Sometimes they were mounted on stands as appears on a fragment of a sarcophagus in the Louvre, where two amorini inspect a dial. In public places they were often mounted on walls or columns, as at Pompeii's Temple of Apollo. Sundials could take many forms as Vitruvius lists (IX, VIII) and vary in size and elaboration. A common type suited to a domestic environment and in Antalya Museum's garden, has had its gnomen restored. Allied to this, a domestic example from Altinum in the Veneto has a solid base, but is enlivened with simple mouldings. The addition of lion's feet to any sundial added a certain style, as can be seen on an example from upper Terracina. Size and elaboration, however, is no indication of whether a dial was intended for public or private use, as a remarkably simple example from the theatre garden at Merida indicates. Alternatively a large and expensive marble lion-footed dial of a different type came from a house in the southern part of Baelo Claudia (Spain). Even more elaborate and surely designed for a garden is a dial from Aquilea with a high base ornamented with roses, acanthus leaves and a sprouting cantharus urn. From Altinum another grand example had a base ornamented with a merchant ship as befitted a port.

Above: A domestic sundial in Antalya Museum's garden.

Left: Venus and a herm on an elaborate sundial from Aquilea and now in the lapidarium of the Archaeological Museum at Udine.

A first-century-AD sundial from Aquilea at the Castle Lapidarium at Udine has, as a base, a statue of Venus resting at a herm – both symbolic of gardens. Acanthus leaves flank Venus while behind her a curling palmette supports the semi-spherical and leaf-fringed dial above. The broken dial still retains lines for the hours VI and VII. Marks on the hexagonal base suggest that it once rested on a pedestal. As goddess of regeneration, Venus suited both domestic and funerary gardens.

Sundials at their simplest did not have to be freestanding objects, but could be built into a wall or even painted on the façade. Such an example in rough stone from Cadiz was stuccoed, with the front painted blue-green and the dial red.

Tintinnabula

The tintinnabulum or wind chime was a bronze inhabitant of porticoes and trees. Often taking the form of the divine winged phallus, or fascinum, the symbol of the deity Fascinus, bells hung from it and their apotropaic tinkle protected against the evil eye and brought prosperity and good fortune. Some tintinnabula aped winged gryphonoid quadrupeds with head, tail, and paws formed as a glans. These echo a relief of a particularly well-endowed creature, complete with collar bell, at Aquilea. An example from Herculaneum depicts a man fighting his own phallus that has taken the form of a lion. Other forms include terracotta bell-shaped humanoid figures whose legs provide clappers and their hooded cloaks the bell. Possibly Alexandrian in origin, examples are in the Merida museum, including a mid-second-century example named Tydides (Diomedes).

Terracotta tintinabula from Merida and in its National Museum of Roman Art. The one on the right is inscribed 'Tydides'.

Domestic Animals in the Garden

Pompeii's House of the Garden of Hercules had a rare example of a dog kennel placed between the summer triclinium and garden shrine. It was roughly constructed from half of a dolium (storage jar) mounted on dwarf walls with the entrance arch formed by the vessel's mouth. Only its ruined walls now survive. This simple solution for housing the household dog was probably commonly employed although rough masonry versions are also known from Pompeii. The fourth-century-AD *Dominus Julius* mosaic from Carthage features a dog outside of a wicker kennel, which would be better suited to the hotter climate

Gravity feeders for birds and other small animals were a surprising addition to some Roman gardens. Looking remarkably like a modern example, a fine terracotta feeder survives at Boscoreale Museum.

CHAPTER 4

Fountains

Fountains provided movement and sound, impressing visitors that the houseowner could afford to be linked to the water mains. A practical consideration for their provision was that the sound of water masked conversation as owners of harems later discovered. For those lacking piped water the recourse was a hand-filled water tower, such as survives at Rabacal, which would gently drain away and could be replenished by slaves. Jets were mostly small and sometimes in the form of lion heads (as at Darenth) for water was thought to spring 'like a lion' from them. Panther, wolf and bear heads were also popular. Most Roman fountains produced only a modest display unless fortunate enough to have a strong natural spring on site as at Woodchester where a jet still shoots several feet into the air. Cantharus/crater-style fountains would only produce an overflowing dome of water within their bowls unless supplied with a central standpipe, occasionally topped, thyrsus-like, with a rose in the form of a pierced pinecone. A bronze standpipe at Merida is covered with pierced pomegranates. Alternatively, the bowls of such fountains were pierced and jets spurted from the sides as with the colossal cantharus in the garden of the Terme Museum in Rome.

Pompeii's House of the Vettii's garden as newly displayed in 1900, featured ivy mounds, various catchment basins, herms on sculptural supports and fountain statuary. (Author's collection)

A Romano-Cretan shell nymph in the Istanbul Archaeological Museum.

Left: A monolithic phallic fountain from the House of the Ocean Gods at Saint-Romain-en-Gal as displayed at its Musée d'Archéologie Nationale.

Below: The massive and superb Tockenham fish spout from the grounds of its substantial villa (and now in store at Devizes Museum) was once the terminal for a Roman water pipe. (Courtesy of David Dawson)

Jets spurted from the sides of pools or aimed at detached stone basins resembling side tables, but with shallow concave tops, as at Pompeii's House of the Vettii. Allied to these were shell nymphs holding scallops before them as catchments for jets. These figures were often bored and provided with pipes themselves. Phallic fountains are known from Saint-Romaine-en-Gal and possibly Chedworth (Inv. 73994). Stylised Hercules clubs or ivy-carved columns were bored to spout water. Paintings at Pompeii and Oplontis show elaborate marble fountains with basins supported by sphinxes and centaurs. At Lausanne-Vidy (Switzerland) a bronze beribboned wreath with many spouts illustrates another form of fountain head.

Fountain statuary might be intended for that purpose or adapted to serve, and crude boring for pipes advertises a secondary use. All manner of subjects could be used although those with rustic, Bacchic, animal or watery allusions were most popular. Venus, Cupid, water nymphs and dolphins abound, but other animals such as serpents, birds and Pegasus occur. Chedworth has a bronze finger from an over-life-sized statue that is oddly interpreted as being reused as a waterspout, although human fountain figures commonly shoot water from their fingers and the site has an impressive nymphaeum. At Corbridge a lion sculpture on a pool coping is generally believed to be reused from a mausoleum, although its mouth appears as designed for a waterspout from the first. Possibly the local sculptor adapted a common design for the commission, although mausolea themselves sometimes included fountains.

Pool culverts often had impressive fountain heads. A lion spout from Aquilea is more than matched by a spectacular fish spout from Tockenham villa in Wiltshire.

Cascade Fountains

Cascade or staircase fountains occur throughout the empire. They were an easy way to imitate the natural splashing waterfall and to add drama to any setting. Monumental cascades at Tivoli included those of the Residence and the curved end of Hadrian's stadium garden. There, eight flights of water stairs divided the cavea as in a theatre, with the seating banks replaced by terraces of planting beds, as at Herod's sunken garden at Jericho. A vomitorium-shaped grotto overlooked the flooded 'orchestra'. Other monumental stair fountains were fed by cisterns on the southern side of the gardens at the Baths of Caracalla in Rome and the theatre-nymphaeum at Baia and nymphaeum of Maecenas at Rome.

Public nymphaea had cascades, and small flights were very popular in domestic situations. Pompeian gardens provide many examples either attached to aediculae wall fountains as at the House of M. Lucretius or as single 'staircase-blocks' mounted by the side of pools as in the House of Meleager. At the House of the Large Fountain water cascaded below a mosaic mask of a river god. Stairs were often topped by a statue, as a main or secondary water source or simply for decoration.

The nymphaeum garden at the House of the Centenary, Pompeii, features a mosaic-covered aedicula and a cascade. Its painted scheme attempts to give one the impression of being on a garden island bordered by a marine canal.

Left: One of a pair of monolithic water stairs from the temple precinct at Silifke, Turkey.

Below: Red and white columns and topiary work surround a blue-painted pool at Pompeii's House of Meleager. Water flowed down stairs from a lost statue and spirted from a central table fountain. A tank next to the cascade either cooled drinks or held fish during cleaning.

A unique marble garden water basin with a miniature staircase may originally have been positioned at an angle. Thessaloniki stone store.

At the House of the Centenary the triclinium faced the peristyle, but was also backed by a nymphaeum garden with a mosaic-covered aedicula and cascade that splashed into a blue-painted pool overlooked by a painted river god. The surrounding murals gave the illusion of a garden island surrounded by a canal with a wider garden beyond. A painted dado trellis sprouting climbing plants was topped (and encircled) by the 'canal' full of marine life, beyond which was a border decorated with sphinx fountains. A ledge here possibly held pot plants to increase the illusion. Behind the sphinxes was a wilderness garden, while a painted game park backed the aedicula.

Stair fountains were incorporated into garden dining. Fine examples occur at the House of the Ephebe, and in the summer biclinium at the Praeda of Julia Felix, where in a room decorated with Nilotic scenes, water flowed down a wall cascade and below the couches to a shallow pool. The temple garden at Silifke, Turkey, had staircase blocks that survived its desolation. Possibly unique is a sink-like marble pool carved from a single block with a miniature staircase preserved at Thessaloniki.

Cascade Blocks

Miniature staircase fountains cut from a single block of stone in a myriad of designs were popular for impluvia and gardens. Often pyramidal and designed to produce a gentle sound of trickling water, a central pipe supplied water to a reservoir on top of the block or a fountain spout above. Holes drilled in the reservoir wall supplied spouts and scallops (a link with nymphaea), or gaps in the rim allowed water to flow down miniature staircases. Some blocks have vertical sides and water may have primarily shot directly into their pools from corner spouts to produce splashing sounds. The British Museum stores an unusual circular example with half-stairs and Bacchic imagery from the Townley Collection. Rome's Terme Museum displays several examples. One, featuring the deities of the week and corner tripods, came from the impluvium of a villa on the Via Anagnina. Unusually, it retains its splash tray. A detached fountain tray survives at Vienne's Lapidarium. Verona's Piazzetta Navona yielded an elegant octagonal fountain with concave, stepped sides and decorated with masks and shell spouts. Its reservoir features a bowl that formed its fountain spout. One from Avenches had its reservoir upheld at the corners by four telamones. Another serving as a holy water stoup in the Cathedral of Concordia Sagittaria, Italy, has spandrels filled with carved water creatures below lion spouts. Dolphins frame its staircases in the manner of theatrical seating banks.

Pompeii's House of Apollo has an octagonal pyramid-cascade originally topped by a figure holding a goose. Its enclosure boasts marble bases for statuettes and an elaborate stepped recticulated inner border, perhaps for pot plants. A fresco of a Diana statue within a lunette basin and a bird-filled orchard once extended the enclosure up the wall. A similar pyramid fountain exists at the House of Loreius Tiburtinus.

In Britain, a stone scallop shell from Halstock villa may have come from one. At Chedworth, a drilled tapering, dome-topped block generally called a 'chimney-vent' may instead be the phallic-like central element of a cascade (Inv. 73994). North Leigh villa has a fountain base allied to cascade blocks. It is somewhat reminiscent of a fountain now in the temple of Augustus at Pula. The deep, square block has semicircular recesses comparable to scallop shells that taper to a collecting circle carved into three sides. The unornamented, narrow back would have been attached to the wall. An inset in the top held the sculpture or urn, which would have been supplied with water from the rear and permitted a constant trickle down to each recess. The reconstruction shows a pierced cantharus fountain with the socle based on one from Great Witcombe, but other sculptural alternatives are possible such as a bronze triple-headed serpent.

A cascade block ornamented with the gods of the week retains its water tray. Now in the Terme Museum, Rome.

Above: An elaborate cascade block now used as a holy water stoup in the cathedral at Concordia Sagittaria.

Right: A reconstruction of the North Leigh villa fountain base to show how it may have functioned. (Author)

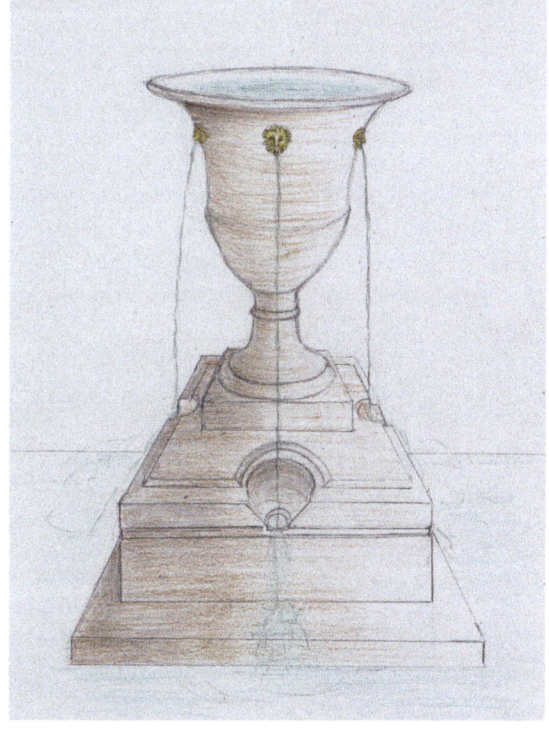

CHAPTER 5

Funerary Gardens

Roman cemeteries lined the roads outside settlements as examples of those at Rome, Pompeii and Aquilea display today. Enclosures might include a funerary garden and cippi were often provided noting the extent of the burial plot. If large enough they provided produce such as wine to serve the needs of the departed, visitors and an income for upkeep or relatives. A remarkable marble slab from the Via Labicana outside of Rome displays the ground plan of a monumental funerary complex together with its buildings and gardens, including the position of 272 shrubs or trees – the latter were probably evergreens, emulating the shady groves of Virgil's Elysium. The outlines of the three-storeyed mausoleum are also shown suggesting a restoration based on other mausolea. Great mausolea like that of Augustus had hanging groves of evergreens. Country residences had their own cemeteries and attached gardens. A fine British villa cemetery may still be seen at Keston, Kent. Those plots containing funnel burials might be furnished with funerary mensae (tables). A pipe descended through their stands, allowing libations to be poured on the ashes. Such a mensa top depicting Venus, goddess of rejuvenation, was discovered at Caerleon. Roman funerals involved feasting and repeat visits at festivals of the dead as portrayed on a lost painting from the Carmona necropolis in Spain. A permanent funerary triclinium was discovered at Pompeii. Its enclosure had garden murals and one should imagine it planted with symbols of immortality and rebirth such as bay laurel and cypress although other plants were considered suitable. Around Narbonne the carline thistle or cardoule had especial significance. It is highly decorative, sun-like and even when dead hardly decays. Villagers still nail it to doors as an apotropaic symbol, but Roman funerary monuments in this

An engraving of a lost painting of a Roman funerary garden banquet on a stibadium couch from Carmona cemetery as recorded in Memorias de la Real Academia de la Historia, 1796. (Author's collection)

A reconstruction of the massive family funerary precinct based on the marble plan from the cemetery beside the Via Labicana outside of Rome. (Author)

The unique and little-known walled funerary precinct of Sidret-el-Balik, near Sabratha, Libya, with masonry stibadia couches, tables and frescoed perimeter wall. (Courtesy of Robert Field)

Amorini threading grape vines on a trellis surrounding the banqueting area at Sidret-el-Balik. (Author)

area also display it as a symbol of immortality. It appears unrecognised in Roman sculpture on metopes and on mosaic pavements where it is called generally called 'acanthus'.

The fourth-century (destroyed AD 365) Libyan funerary garden of Sidret-el-Balik is a unique survival, with 180 square metres of frescoes and four plastered stibadia couches, tables, tomb and chapel. The enclosure's frescoes depict a paradeisos garden, country and hunting scenes. Amorini pick grapes from a trellis while roses decorate the couches and garland the mausoleum. An awning probably shielded the diners from the sun and a pool provided water.

A villa with a colonnaded portico, overhead vine treuis and an attached arched nymphaeum from Sidret-el Balik cemetery garden.

CHAPTER 6

The Palatine Gardens

The ceilings of the palace rest on columns that cannot be counted
And the cross-beams glitter brightly, coated in Dalmatian gold.
Coolness drops from the shade where ancient trees arrest
The heat, and sparkling fountains jump in marble ponds.
Here Nature obeys no seasons; the Dog-Star chills,
Winter warms, and the house conforms the year to its wishes.

Statius, *Occasional Poems* (1.2.152–157)

It is difficult to know whether the palace gardens on Rome's Palatine Hill were innovative or followed and developed existing fashion. That they evolved is clear from additions and alterations made to those in the Domus Augustana. Those of the Augustan period were apparently limited to the relatively small peristyles of the imperial houses. A house at the Vigna Barberini had a peristyle garden flanked by parallel pools. The early palaces included the hanging gardens of the Domus Tiberiana laid over the palace's vaulted platform, and a pair of oval fishponds believed to date from Tiberius' reign. Nero's Golden House had huge gardens, once assumed to be naturalistically landscaped, but now imagined as divided into more formal

One of the fishponds
of Tiberius' palace
on the Palatine
as excavated
around 1880.
(Author's collection)

47

Tiberius' palace with the fishponds. A model prepared for the 2001 exhibition 'Il Giardino Dei Cesari' at the Terme Museum, Rome, illustrating the French School of Rome's investigative work on the Palatine between 1985 and 1999.

spaces. By the time that Domitian's huge palace was built in the AD 90s, gardens 'with ancient trees' linked the buildings, were integrated with the architecture and were lavishly adorned with sculpture, fountains and water features.

The Water Labyrinth of the First Peristyle

The unicursal labyrinth was greatly employed by Roman designers. On mosaics it took the form of four interlinked classical labyrinths around a central panel. It could also be employed in water gardens. In the Domus Flavia the great peristyle garden court fronting the state triclinium was filled by a huge pool with a rhythmically niched border designed to delight by its pattern of light and shade and to provide shelter for fish. In the centre an octagonal island was surrounded by a labyrinth of opus signinum lined water channels and fountains that was possibly a secondary feature. Theseus and the Minotaur often occupy the centre on labyrinth mosaics; possibly, they formed a fountain group on the island. At the farthest extreme from such magnificence is a single block cut with a circular classical labyrinth from a domestic

The great labyrinth garden pool of the Palatine's Domus Flavia.

A Roman water maze from a domestic garden in Manisa, Turkey.

garden in Manisa, Turkey. Water flowed in from one side and, on reaching the centre, was reversed down parallel circular channels to an outlet on the opposite side – a clever and pleasing conceit.

The Nymphaea Fountains

The imperial triclinium or Cenatio Iovis faced the labyrinth garden, but was also flanked by two massive oval marble-clad nymphaea fountains within attached peristyles, which diners could also view through six great windows. Set within oval, column-fringed pools, the tiered fountains featured at least one terrace of fountain statues within niches above an upper water channel. One restored fountain survives. Where achievable, this idea of surrounding diners with prospects of natural and artificial beauty and called Cyzicene triclinia after those in the town

The restored surviving core of one of two nymphaea fountains that stood either side of the Cenatio Iovis.

A water garden to the side of a triclinium at Italica's House of the Birds.

of Cyzicus, Anatolia, is found throughout the empire. The House of the Triumph of Neptune at Acholla (Tunisia) and the House of the Birds at Italica (Spain) are but two.

The Peltae Garden of the Sunken Peristyle

A striking water garden filled the sunken peristyle of the Domus Augustana, fronting a suite of state chambers. Again, designed like a mosaic with confronted peltae (Amazons' shields) islands, it was obviously intended to be spectacular when viewed from both above and below. Probably Hadrianic in date, it aggrandised an earlier rectangular island perhaps used for alfresco dining. At basement level it was designed to be viewed from the suite's main chamber on the north-west side of the courtyard. From there the geometry of the islands would not show to advantage and so its major decorative effect was probably achieved by a combination of fountains, statuary and mosaic. Plantings were possibly minimal. The corners of the design were likely filled by pedestals bearing colossal statuary, urns or statues on columns that would be on a level with the upper floor. The reconstruction peoples the islands with a Helicon cycle featuring a central Pegasus fountain. Only Conimbriga's House of the Fountains' garden and Olympia's Leonidaion approach the extent and complexity of this ensemble. Recent research suggests that the basement rooms are early Flavian in date and the upper rooms and gallery Hadrianic. Before these additions the basement rooms were topped by a hanging garden or terrace. Around AD 300 six narrow rectangular basins, connected to the main pool and crossed by bridges, were cut into the peristyle floor.

An impression of the Sunken Peristyle in the Domus Augustana as it might have appeared in Hadrianic times. (Author)

Reflecting Pools

The Hadrianic extensions to the Domus Augustana included the insertion of three white marble-lined fountain-pools into basement gardens where they reflected light through the huge windows and cooled the air. Two are identical in shape being rectangular, but rhythmically indented on all sides by rectangular and semicircular niches from which fountains played. One has a cascade. Another rectangular pool (later converted to a natatio) is headed by a nymphaeum within its peristyle. Courtyards filled by large water features are particularly popular in North Africa. Volubilis' House of the Columns has a large circular basin filling its peristyle. Plants

One of the Hadrianic reflecting pools outside the basement chambers of the Domus Augustana.

grew in the spandrels. Timgad's House of the Piscina's deep apsidal pool is raised within the walls of its surrounding colonnade.

The Upper Peristyle Garden of the Domus Augustana

The Upper Peristyle's large apsidal marble-clad fishpond was bordered by a garden and additional fountains. Elegant suites of rooms surrounded it. The pool's borders were rhythmically indented with lunettes and rectangular niches as well as V shapes. Fountains lined the sides and marine-themed sculpture is believed to have stood in the water. Much sculpture was discovered here during excavation. Around 300 AD an arched 'harbour-mole' was added, leading to a rectangular island with a building generally reconstructed as a small temple. What has not been considered is that it led to a garden building based on a pharos, a structure found at the end of such moles, which would have been a charming addition to this playful 'seascape'.

The Upper Peristyle water garden with its mole and island. The Sunken Peristyle is beyond.

The Hippodrome/Stadium Garden

The pleasing conceit of gardens and pools aping the shape of the hippodrome or circus occurs throughout the Roman world. Pliny (5.6) waxes lyrical about his circus garden in the letter describing his villa in Tuscany. The hippodrome garden par excellence was that of the Domus Augustana on the Palatine, dating to around AD 92 and possibly designed by the architect Rabirius. Headed at the north end by a huge nymphaeum, this sunken garden had semicircular nymphaea pools at each end aping the metae in a real circus, and was surrounded by a two-storey peristyle. Originally, like the sunken peristyle, this was single storeyed with either a terrace or

The Hippodrome garden as first designed with a hanging garden and imagined by G. Tognetti around 1900. (Author's collection)

hanging garden over the lower arcade. The outer path was intended for promenading on foot or by litter and even a carriage according to Martial (1.12.82) and Juvenal (8.178). Lavishly decorated and full of sculpture, many fragments are now in the Palatine Antiquarium. A long vegetal and sculptural spina possibly joined the two pools. Domitian liked this style of garden and it was duplicated at the Albanum Domitiani, his villa in the Alban hills. Hadrian's version at Tivoli kept the general shape, but divided it into three sections filled with pools, pavilions and fountains. At Silin, Libya, the maritime Villa of the Small Circus has a western garden with a long, narrow, spina-like central flower bed featuring an off-centre pool. At either end were semicircular basins. It is possible such gardens, especially when connected with baths and palaestrae, were equipped with miniature metae and were the scene of the 'circus game' played by young men and women. This involved propelling a pair of toy chariot wheels on rods around a miniature spina, as appears on the Great Palace mosaic in Istanbul. A female champion of the sport appears on the 'bikini girls' mosaic at Piazza Armerina in Sicily. The long palaestra or garden of Conimbriga's Trajanic baths, which overlooked the spectacular Rio dos Mouros gorge, may have featured a hippodrome garden. It was reached by a grand staircase and at each end sported a pair of exedrae either side of a central fountain pool. The praetoria at Vetera I (Xanten) and Caerleon had long apsidal hippodrome gardens, and the monumental water garden at Welschbillig, near Trier, with its circus-inspired balustrading, central spina and metae fountains, must also be included. Boat races possibly took place there, around its spina. A huge banqueting room spanned the north-east

An Interpretative reconstruction of the hippodrome water garden at Welschbillig, Germany. (Author)

end of the pool, perhaps inspired by Hadrian's Serapaeum at Tivoli. In London the garden court of the Governor's Palace, that enigmatic monumental complex on Thameside, with its long apsidal pool, may perhaps be classified as one.

The Hanging Water Garden

Investigations since the 1970s have shown that one of the great arcaded platforms of the Domus Severiana stretching from the hippodrome garden is Flavian in date. Its two-storey substructure was raised to the ground level of the Domus Augustana and a villa-like wing with two apses entered from the first floor of the hippodrome opened on to a vast hanging water basin that topped the platform. Light wells, perhaps ornamented with sculpture, spaced along the basin protruding from the water. Colonnaded ambulatories surrounded the terrace overlooking the Circus Maximus and beyond. For those within the 'villa', the view across the waters and through the colonnades must have been remarkable.

An interpretative reconstruction of the Palatine's hanging water garden after the work of Legnyel Toulouse Architekten, based on the model of A. Müller of Architekturreferat DAI Berlin. (Author)

The Great Garden and the Adonaea

By early Flavian times a great 135 by 165 metre horseshoe-shaped hanging garden with surrounding multistoreyed porticoes had been constructed on 17-metre-high vaults overlooking the Colosseum valley in the area later called Vigna Barberini. It incorporated the foundations of Nero's revolving dining room. Fountains and statues interspersed with shrubs were spaced around the garden's perimeter and a shallow white marble canal ran in front of the porticoes. A small grove and paths divided up the interior. Hadrian remodelled the northern edge and added fountains and sculpture. The great fire of AD 191 damaged its western side and either demolition or drastic alterations followed (or were intended) under Severus, but the gardens later made way for Elagabalus' Heliogabalium.

The Adonaea or Gardens of Adonis are partially known from Fragments 46a–d of the Forma Urbis Roma, the ancient marble map of Rome. They feature a euripus canal surrounded by niched flower beds. Fragment 68ab, featuring a shallow exedra, may have belonged to it. On each side four lines of bedding trenches or hedges ran parallel with the euripus and were cut by central paths. Five to seven rows of planting pits for shrubs or trees are shown top and bottom, and five at the sides. The garden's location is unknown and a site on the Campus Martius has been proposed. A passage in Philostratus' *Life of Apollonius* (Apoll. 7.32) where the teacher-cum-magician meets Domitian has suggested to others that it was on the Palatine: 'And the Emperor was wearing a wreath of olive leaves, for he had just been offering a sacrifice to Athena in the hall of Adonis and this hall was bright with baskets of flowers, such as the Syrians at the time of the festival of Adonis make up in his honour, growing them under their very roofs.' This is alternatively interpreted as a smaller, mobile garden. Tradition placed this garden of potted plants and the site of the annual Adonis festival at the Vigna Barberini, but the sunken peristyle's stateroom has also been suggested.

A model of the Palatine's Great Garden made for the exhibition 'Il Giardino dei Cesari' at the Terme Museum, Rome, in 2001.

A mosaic from Daphne (Harbiye), Turkey, showing a garlanded young man with pot plants, possibly celebrating the Adonia.

In Athens the Adonia was celebrated by women. They planted lettuce and fennel seeds in pots called 'Gardens of Adonis', which sprouted before withering and dying. Variations of the celebrations occurred throughout the Mediterranean and Philostratus' reference suggests that the Roman version was more floral. A mosaic from Daphne (Harbiye) in Turkey depicts a young man holding a pot plant, possibly illustrating the Adonis celebration. Another pot plant is displayed on a column behind him.

The dating and site of the later temple in the middle of the terrace creates more problems as it is generally believed that Elagabalus adapted an existing temple for his Heliogabalium. The objection to placing the Adonaea on the site, however, collapses if the temple was newly built as possibly the marble plan records either an incomplete garden or an ultimately unfinished Severan project.

The Heliogabalium

Whatever the origins of this temple, recent excavation disclosed that it had a paved courtyard and a cella flanked by three long planting beds, irrigated by underground channels, and rows of keyhole plantings. Many planting pots were discovered and it is suggested that shrubs and small trees filled the beds. Following the death of Elagabalus the temple was rededicated to Jupiter Ultor.

Mosaics and Gardens

There is a direct correlation between the geometric designs used for island water gardens (and possibly flower beds) and those used on mosaics. Sometimes just elements are used, but other gardens are exact copies of standard floor designs. The Palatine sunken garden's peltae design occurs either as single mosaic panels or as one of a series of patterns, as at the Marine Baths at Sabratha, Libya. The four-lunette-indented square island found at Conimbriga's houses of the Fountains and Cantaber, and Vila Cardilio, appears on mosaics such as at Loupian, France, where cantharus fountains occupy each lunette pool. Likewise, the Palatine's water labyrinth is inspired by mosaic designs. At Olympia, the Leonidaion's cushion-shaped island aped the design found on mosaics such as at Brislington Villa in Bristol.

This correlation between mosaics and gardens is reversed in the desire to bring into the house the stylised mosaic representations of gardens and fountain pools. Mosaic fish pools

A panel from a geometric mosaic in the Marine Baths at Sabratha, Libya, that matches the design of the Sunken Peristyle's islands, with an ochre four-lunette-indented-square and grey and black peltae.

A symbolic mosaic water garden from the centre of the Augst Gladiator mosaic. A round central fountain pool with fishes has planted spandrels. Two rectangular pools at either end hold lotus buds and seed heads.

A small but fabulous Roman atrium garden from Chamaretou Street, Sparta. Lavishly adorned with mosaic, it has a raised central octagonal fountain pool surrounded by a planting trench (here excavated) that is itself surrounded by an octagonal enclosure wall. (Courtesy of Anastasia Panagiotopolou)

A rare 1903 photograph of the excavation of the garden of the Villa of the Aviary at Carthage. An octagonal flower bed is surrounded by a mosaic covered with animals and birds, leaves and branches. Each spandrel held a stone frame for a living tree. (Author's collection)

Mosaic-covered walls surrounding garden beds at the Villa Silene, Libya.

are symbolic of the desire for status achieved by the real thing. The triclinium at Volubilis' Orpheus House has a rectangular central mosaic pool holding nine dolphins. The *Gladiator Mosaic* at Augst, Switzerland, floors a reception room overlooking the garden peristyle. Viewed from its west end, a swastika meander encompasses six gladiatorial panels and represents a peristyle floor surrounding a central rectangular mosaic 'water-garden'. This contains a guilloche-bordered circular 'pool' containing a cantharus fountain and fish. The adjoining spandrels represent triangular garden beds and are decorated with rose bushes and trailing plants. 'Pools' at either end hold lotus flower buds and seed heads. The lotus/water lily was an extremely popular motif in Roman mosaics, but particularly on Romano-British ones. Its bud, leaf and flower appear everywhere. Its leaf is often confused with that of the ivy on mosaics as both are similar in Roman art. Venus' lotus symbolised rebirth, opening and closing with the day and born each spring from the mud. Such mosaics as that at the Verulamium Park hypocaust should be interpreted as resembling a lotus pool. A mosaic from Daphni, Turkey, has naturalistic panels depicting lotus and river fowl surrounded by bands of zig-zag – one of the artistic conventions for portraying water in mosaic.

Peristyle islands surrounded by a canal are linked to a second-century-AD mosaic in Lyons, remarkable for depicting sea creatures in the water. The connection between mosaics and water gardens seems particularly strong in Northern Provinces, where winter frosts made elaborate outside water features and fountains problematic. Symbolic mosaic water gardens and fountain depictions are often found – hence at Frampton, Kingscote and Hemsworth, Venus appears in symbolic pools accompanied by sea creatures or lotus flowers. At Woodchester, Orpheus plays next to a central fountain pool once patterned with fish and encircled by animals and an acanthus hedge, beyond which water nymphs sport in their pools. This recalls the fountain circling and statue-filled garden beds of Pompeii's House of M. Lucretius.

A remarkable garden based on a mosaic design, but incorporating mosaics and plants, comes from Chamaretou Street, Sparta. In a sumptuously adapted atrium, the centre of the garden had a raised mosaic-covered octagonal island pool featuring a central guilloche-bordered square surrounded by sea beasts and holding a small fountain. A low rim contained the shallow pool. Flower beds surrounded the island, bounded by a low mosaic-covered outer wall – itself forming an irregular octagon with cutaway corners. Each of these concave corners held an apotropaic mosaic gorgoneion. This juxtaposing of mosaic and living nature has been noted elsewhere in Carthage's Villa of the Aviary.

Mosaics were also used as minor decorative additions to garden beds although few remain. The island beds of Conimbriga's House of the Fountains retained one fragment to show that their edges were shouldered with mosaic featuring a running lotus or ivy leaf design. Likewise the dwarf walls surrounding the long garden beds of the maritime Villa Silene (Sileen), Libya, are topped with mosaics featuring a peopled vegetal scroll. The sloping shoulders of these walls have symbolic zig-zag water patterns alluding to the fact that the garden beds were surrounded by irrigation channels.

Above: A model of the Roman garden in the peristyle of the Leonidaion at Olympia displayed in the site museum.

Right: Silenus relaxes in the hexagonal shade of four great vines growing from canthrai at the corners of a mosaic at EL Jem echoing the garden of Carthageis Villa of the Aviary.

CHAPTER 7

Water Gardens with Geometric Islands

Peristyle gardens often had a bordering canal. At Olympia the Roman aggrandisement of the Leonidaion's square peristyle garden produced a complex design. The four corners of the great peristyle held concave, triangular, flower beds bordered by a wide and deep canal that surrounded a cushion-shaped 'square' island. The latter's concave sides were topped by four rectangular, concave-sided and triangular-ended flower beds now planted with oleanders. The 'cushion's' rounded corners probably held statuary. Within the 'cushion' island was a circular canal that provided an inner concave edge to the flower beds. This inner canal bordered a central circular island with a fountain. Apart from the flower beds all was covered in marble or mosaic.

Sometimes canals surrounded three sides of the garden as in the trapezoidal peristyle of Merida's House of the Amphitheatre, or turned the garden into an island as at its House of the Mithraeum. The larger squared plots may have been used for alfresco dining as at St-Romain-en-Gal's House of the Ocean Gods and the House of the Columns. Both sported pergolas. Some small islands had rhythmically niched edges as at the House of the Cascade, Utica or the House of Hercules, Volubilis. Four circular islands sat in the deep pool filling the entire peristyle at La Estación villa, Malaga.

An island garden at the House of the Mithraeum, Merida.

Surrounded by water on three sides, a pergola sheltered a summer triclinium and its pool at the House of the Ocean Gods at Saint-Romain-en-Gal. Diners faced a nymphaeum off to the left.

The summer triclinium of the House of the Columns at Saint-Romain-en-Gal with its pergola and three fountain niches.

The rhythmically niched flower bed of the garden pool of the House of Hercules, Volubilis. The outer pool wall reverses the usual indented square design. (Courtesy of Corinne Board)

Conimbriga, Portugal

Conimbriga's water gardens rival those of the Palatine in complexity. Lack of comparative evidence prevents one from claiming that their geometric islands are unique, but they seem unmatched thus far, with only that of Olympia's Leonidaion approaching.

The second century AD saw the construction of most of Conimbriga's great houses. However, around AD 300 the worrying military and political situation prompted the building of a contracted fortification circuit. Properties in the path of the new wall were demolished. The palatial House of Cantaber was spared. Flavian in origins, it grew over the centuries occupying a complete insula. Its central peristyle (on the visual axis with the principal entrance) framed a water garden with large L-shaped island flower beds with opposed niches on their short sides. Surrounded by water, the islands visually formed a rectangular central pool surrounded by four circular pools. An adjacent peristyle edged with planting troughs and a pool refreshed eastern chambers. To the west the service area had another peristyle with a small rectangular pool. The Cyzicene triclinium's three huge windows permitted views across a trio of surrounding pools and (through its doors) to the central garden and the principal entrance. The pools on the south and west sides were rectangular, surrounded by planters or platforms for pot plants. The large eastern one had rhythmically niched edges similar to two Hadrianic light-well pools in the Palatine's Domus Augustana. Deep planters between the niches permitted large shrubs or small trees to be grown. To the south, the triclinium overlooked a pool and garden beyond that filled the rest of the insula. It later made way for expanded baths. The new town wall was built hard against the house and a charming suite of rooms were added in the space between. A peristyle and water garden with island beds and a fountain were constructed. Four roughly L-shaped islands framed a central octagonal fountain pool flanked by two four-lunetted square

The peristyle water garden of Conimbriga's House of Cantaber, looking from the atrium to the triclinium.

The design of the eastern pool beside the triclinium window at the House of Cantaber copies the reflecting pools on the Palatine. Anciently projections into the rhythmically niched pool contained earth-filled planters.

island beds, based on mosaic design. A similar but large rectangular-lunetted island filled the peristyle at Villa el Santiscal (Arcos De La Frontera), Portugal. There fountains played in the lunettes as on Loupian's mosaic.

Several relatively new houses made way for the late fortification circuit. The House of the Skeletons (named for the necropolis that succeeded it), displays the care with which the visual axis of its layout was planned. Those entering the atrium looked directly across the water garden to the centrally placed triclinium beyond and vice versa. A rill encircled most of the rectangular central flower bed that was indented and enlivened with a small lunette facing the entrance. The idea of enhancing the important views of an otherwise straight-sided island by the addition of a lunette is widely used in Roman gardens. The Houses of the Mithraeum and the Amphitheatre, Merida, have such lunettes facing their triclinia. Outside the triclinium diners viewed a separate square pool with a pot-plant shelf that was cut into the island. On its south side the island has a rectangular protrusion – perhaps for a garden sculpture.

The fourth-century-AD private suite built against the town wall featured a peristyle and water garden that included indented, niched squares, as on the Palatine.

A view from the atrium across the garden to the triclinum at the House of the Skeletons. Water almost surrounded the garden and the view of the front wall from the entrance was enlivened with a niche.

The House of the Swastika's quadrant flower bed islands are linked on the pool's visually important sides by niched walls. The three doors of the triclinium appear opposite.

Another victim of the town wall was the House of the Swastikas, named after the good luck symbol found on its triclinium mosaic. The house had a long history and had been altered over the years. This resulted in the visual axis being slightly off-centre and diners in its triclinium not having the usual clear view of the water garden, although three doors opened onto its peristyle. The water garden was based on a mosaic design with island spandrels linked by lunette-shaped walls.

The second-century House of the Fountains, with its over 500 fountain jets, moulded stucco, mural paintings and 569.03 square metres of mosaic, was the wall's most spectacular victim. Its water garden is the largest and most elaborate known beyond the Palatine. The pool's concrete flower beds originally had lotus-scroll mosaic borders, of which only a fragment remained when excavated, but all of the original pipework was intact that had been fed by the nearby aqueduct and so, in consolidation, it was possible to make the fountains work again. Box edging was planted, but has now been removed. The house's visual axis again looked from the entrance hall across the water garden with its six islands, through the triclinium and to a garden beyond. The four islands at the ends of the great pool are L-shaped with lunette ends and resemble those of the Cantaber House. The large central ones have lunettes on three sides. Together the islands form a rhythmically niched central water path down the visual axis of the pond like the central approach path at Fishbourne Palace. The surrounding peristyle mosaics are more elaborate on the southern side, suggesting that guests were led along that ceremonial route, over the roundels portraying the victorious heroes Perseus and Bellerophon, and past a richly decorated exedra. They would then be led to the mosaic-carpeted Cyzicene triclinium. Here diners could look down the water garden or through three great windows at the rear and sides into the back garden or orchard. A deep fishpond surrounded the triclinium on three sides, a design echoing that surrounding the Temple of Diana at Evora. Pipes in the fishpond's sides provided spawning grounds for fish, although the pool would have also been suitable for swimming. North of the triclinium, chambers opened on to another peristyle and a small water garden with a lunetteed square island. South of the central water garden, rooms were ranged around a private peristyle with a pool and nymphaeum.

The peristyle water garden of Conimbriga's House of the Fountain looking towards the triclinium. The most elaborate known outside of the Palatine, it contains over 500 working fountain jets.

The aspect from the triclinium looking down the garden's ceremonial water avenue towards the atrium and the fortification wall beyond.

The fishpond clasping the walls of the triclinium of the House of the Fountains. Originally great windows provided diners with views on each side.

CHAPTER 8

Nymphaea

The word 'nymphaeum' embraces and is used to describe various things – from grottoes to lunette pools, shrines and public fountains. Water and its nymphs, often combined with elaborate decoration, connects all.

The natural grotto at Sperlonga, Italy, with its seaside cavern and theatrical Odyssean sculptural displays, including Scylla and the blinding of Polyphemus, obviously had great influence. It was artificially recreated by Domitian at Castelgandolfo and possibly at Hadrian's Serapeum. The Odyssean theme appears widely, including in Claudius' triclinium grotto at Baia. The connection of dining with grottoes was strong, and summer dining grottoes were created in hillsides. Monumental dining nymphaea, such as the so-called Temple of Minerva Medici in the

The grotto of Tiberius at the maritime villa of Sperlonga. The central island held a summer triclinium surrounded by a rectangular marine fish tank.

Reconstruction of the huge Blinding of Polyphemus group from the rear of the Sperlonga grotto juxtaposed with original fragments.

Horti Liciniani on the Esquiline Hill, decorated the great private gardens of Rome and a huge nymphaeum stood at the end of the Palatine's hippodrome garden.

Screen nymphaea ornamented Rome's gardens and streets. The Horti Aciliani on the Pincio possessed a fabulous 326.70-metre-diameter semicircular nymphaeum, while Nero transformed the platform of the Temple of the Divine Claudius into a nymphaeum of extraordinary length and grandeur to improve the prospect from his Golden House.

Stabiae's San Marco villa possessed a curved nymphaeum at the end of its swimming pool. The north-west end of Caerleon's natatio had an elaborate 9-metre-high nymphaeum with a fountain sculpture of a dolphin and Venus, ancestor of Augustus, the founder of the 2nd Augustan Legion. This nymphaeum was an aggrandisement of such Pompeian nymphaea as that in the House of the Grand Duke of Tuscany. As ancestress of the Julian family, Venus was particularly pertinent. Long pools headed by freestanding nymphaea are uncommon. At Timgad a temple to Dea Patria overlooks the long 22 by 7 metre pool, while at Perge a public nymphaeum heads the 'Canopic' pools running centrally down the street. Domestically a large detached nymphaeum heads a mosaic lined canal at El Jem's House of Africa and modestly at the House of Loreius Tiburtinus, Pompeii. Near Evora, Portugal, the villa at Tourega had a reservoir-cum-natatio 24.5 by 4.6 metres headed by a small square, tank-like nymphaeum. Aesthetically the idea of a canal headed by a nymphaeum finds its apogee in Hadrian's Canopus and Serapaeum and at Tivoli.

Chedworth possessed a nymphaeum, and three other religious buildings in its hinterland. The author's investigations indicate that a fragment of a curving run of large-scale S cresting, denoting a sacred structure, matches the curve of the shrine's apse, suggesting that it was

Two fragmentary statues incorporating fern leaf decoration found outside of Room 5A may originally have stood on the fronting pedestals of the nymphaeum. (Author)

open to the sky. This open nymphaeum broadly resembles that of the nymph Egeria at Nemi. A second- to third-century terracotta Venus from Quai Arloing, Lyons, depicts such an open structure with S-cresting, but is obfuscated by the problems of depicting perspective in its modelling. A small nymphaeum also stood on the terraces at Groundwell Ridge, Swindon.

Decorating the Pool

Garden pools were often painted blue or lined with marble and mosaic. Mosaic depictions of Oceanus, fish, fishermen, boats or a zig-zag water motif are found. This suggests regular cleaning was undertaken or a constant flow of water was present as excavators have remarked on the lack of silt in some pools. Certainly pools might have metal or terracotta filters fitted or, as at Chedworth and Keynsham, pipes may have been connected to stone settling tanks for water distribution.

Lunette and Square Nymphaea Pools

The lunette nymphaeum pool was popular from the first century AD. Often positioned in front of a major reception room, the visual axis passed over it and took the viewer into the garden. Its fountains cooled the air and added sound and movement. In warm climates the rear wall was left low, matching that of the peristyle so as not to impede the view, but, when part of an enclosed corridor, it would have been of ceiling height and pierced by windows, allowing views

Prospect from the triclinium of the House of the Cascade, Utica looking over the lunette nymphaeum pool towards the sundial on the peristlye pool's island.

Subterranean lunette pool looking into the light-well garden in the House of the Fishing at Bulla Regia, Tunisia.

Marine fishpool with a fishing amorino in the lunette pool at the House of the Cascade, Utica.

of the garden beyond. Lunettes were particularly popular in North African provinces and many examples survive. Some were completely surrounded by walls while others were only walled on the curve and the straight front closed by slabs. In sun-baked Bulla Regia (Tunisia) the cool summer basement rooms of the House of the Fishing were provided with an elaborate lunette pool that led off of a reception room and into a small light-well garden. The curved wall was corrugated with alternating niches; its mosaic-covered sloping top featured fishing amorini. Mosaic also lined the sides surrounding an opus sectile pool bottom. Five holes in the top of the curve either once housed fountain jets or were planted with vines and a trellis. At Utica the House of the Figured Basin featured a lunette, with the rear wall decorated with a mosaic of rose bushes and two female figures flanking an armed male. Below this was a border of marble and the basin was floored with a water-pattern mosaic. Also in Utica the visual axis of the triclinium of the House of the Cascade opened onto a lunette, beyond which was the peristyle garden's rhythmically indented island. A mosaic of fish and an amorino fishing floored the lunette; with water agitated by a fountain, the mosaic fish would have appeared to move. Oceanus appears on some pool bottoms peering through the waters. Beautiful lunettes featuring him have been found at Sousse, Acholla, Carthage and Thuburbo Maius.

In Europe, although mosaic-covered lunettes occur (such as at Milreu, Portugal), fear of frost determined that marble or opus signinum was used instead. Symbolic pools in mosaic regularly appear. The Spanish villa at Carranque featured a mosaic trompe l'oeil lunette pool in an apse of the north corridor opposite the triclinium. An Oceanus with a beard of rolling waves, accompanied by marine denizens, dominated this apse. A hole in the skirting has suggested the presence of a fountain here, but it would have covered the mosaic and the gap is rather an outlet to drain water from washing the floor. At Verulamium the famous scallop-shell mosaic projecting into the garden outside of the triclinium at House I, Insula II, was surely another symbolic pool, as at Carranque, with windows above providing views of the garden beyond.

Mike Codd's reconstruction of the town house with a nymphaeum pool found at Vine Street, Leicester. Later research has suggested that the peristyle garden was only crossed by paths and not completely gravelled as pictured here. (Courtesy of Richard Buckley and ULAS)

Brading villa's garden nymphaeum showing the later inner wall. The restored line of the water pipe approaches from the top left. Originally the fountain stone would have been set higher up the wall. (Courtesy of David Reeves)

At Nennig, Germany, a lunette pool faced a central reception room in the northern internal peristyle. Another, in the courtyard of Cologne's House of the Dionysus Mosaic, was part of an elaborate nymphaeum composed of planters, pools of varying depth and a fountain. In Britain a lunette has been found at Wall in the peristyle of the second-century mansio. Here it backed the entrance hall with the view of the peristyle behind it. A courtyard house at Berkeley Street, Gloucester (Insula I), had a substantial lunette facing a triclinium. It projected into the partially paved courtyard as a three-sided apse. A house at Vine Street, Leicester, had a nymphaeum fronting the principal reception room in the north range, enhancing the view to the central garden. The garden was covered with thick dark soil. Clay and concrete patches suggest a garden crossed by paths rather than a totally surfaced area as originally restored. A possible orchard or kitchen garden behind the house (enclosed by a boundary wall) held a circular stone-built well. At Arbeia, South Shields, the courtyard of the commanding officer's house had a square room with a pool replaced by an apsidal one. Both are interpreted as cold plunges attached to a bath suite rather than nymphaea. Recent excavations at Chedworth show that the square room attached to Room 25b was a nymphaeum pool. It drained to the east, possibly connecting with the spout and tank discovered beyond the cross-corridor in 2018. Windows would have permitted views of the courtyard garden and for those outside to have viewed the postulated statue that was the focus of 25b. Other porch-like rooms outside main reception rooms in Romano-British domestic architecture may also have been square nymphaea or symbolic ones if floored with mosaics with an aquatic or fountain theme. At Brading a covered lunette pool was attached to the west boundary wall of the villa as a true garden nymphaeum, floored with tile and constructed of opus signinum-covered limestone blocks. In 2005, while identifying architectural stonework on-site for the villa, the author discovered a bored limestone block, once inset with a bronze fountain spout. This block has now been placed on the lunette. Its front wall was later broadened with an inner length, leading to the conclusion that it was blocked off and abandoned. However, as both walls survived to the same height this addition may have been to facilitate reaching across to the fountain spout. The 'boundary wall' building at Littlecote resembles that at Brading, but was robbed out and seemingly lacked a watercourse.

Circular Pools

Circular pools do not appear to have been popular. Volubilis' House of the Columns has a uniquely large example filling its peristyle with only the spandrels planted. Périgueux's Vesunna Domus' peristyle features one and Narbonne's House of the Porticoes has another lined with opus spicatum. Pompeii's House of the Hunt has one painted blue and others occur

The pool garden of the House of the Columns at Volubilis, Morocco. The spandrels of the peristyle would have been planted. (Author's collection)

at the House of M. Lucretius and the House of Apollo. Baia's nymphaeum theatre features an example, and a sacred circular natatio survives at Heliopolis (Hammam Berda), Algeria.

Rectangular and Euripus Pools

Rectangular pools are the most commonly encountered. They can be completely plain or aggrandised with niches or apsidal decoration. Elongated versions are sometimes called a Canopus canal after the branch of the Nile that linked Alexandria with Abukir. Those that are long and narrow like the octagonally ended pool in the 'Libraries Garden' at Hadrian's Tivoli villa are called 'euripus' after the narrow Euripus Strait or the name used for the circus' central spina. To possess pools in areas where water was scarce was to flaunt one's wealth and influence. Hence both the House of Lucius Verus and the House of Africa at Thysdrus (El Jem) in Tunisia would have impressed contemporaries in a way that is hard for the modern viewer to comprehend. Utica's spectacular House of the Oecus' garden had a lunette pool and a euripus with lunette pools either end fronting the two main rooms. Piazza Armerina's pool also featured end lunettes and semicircular side bays. At the villa of the Nonii Arrii, Toscolano, on Lake Garda the inner walls of an enormous 47 by 6 metre rectangular fountain basin had alternating rectangular and semicircular niches, while corner angles were also niched and circular swellings near each end of the canal compromised its rectangularity. These surrounded lunette-shaped islands intended for sculpture. This pool was built solely to display the family's wealth as the villa it fronted already looked out over Lake Garda. The Villa of the Papyri at Herculaneum had an elegant canal with ends featuring shouldered lunettes. The design stayed popular throughout

The euripus with octagonal fountain terminals at the Libraries' Garden Hadrian's villa, Tivoli.

The great pool as reconstructed on the model of the villa at Echternach in the site museum.

the Roman era. The villa of Pisoes, Portugal, boasted its own dam that supplied the villa with water. Its rectangular pool was 40 by 8.30 metres long and the baths featured an open-air 6 by 4.6 metre natatio. Rectangular pools were popular in the gardens of Vaison-la-Romaine (France). At the House of the Dolphins and another in Place de Monfort, long pools fronted the garden façades. Both had three lunettes on the garden side, which in the first house were divided off into separate pools, one of which was later planted. The House of the Silver Bust and that of Apollo both had plain canals fronting principal rooms.

The rectangular pool is commonly encountered in the Northern Provinces, possibly stemming from the fear of frost damage on an elaborate structure. They could be huge, however. The palatial villa of Echternach in Luxembourg possessed an enormous pool, 59 by 14.5 metres, which fronted the main range of building. Luxembourg's huge villa, Marisca at Mersch, boasted an even longer apsidal ended one at 75.6 by 6.5 metres. Near Trier, the great fourth-century pool at the villa of Welschbillig sat on an axis with the main complex and a banqueting house.

In Britain several complexes featured rectangular pools. The earliest known is at the palatial Eccles villa in Kent dated to AD 65–120. Running parallel with the villa's front corridor, it measured internally 24.9 by 3.45 metres. It was demolished around AD 180 and a pedestal or garden sculpture was erected on its south-east wall. At Halstock Villa in Dorset, the elaborate system of culverts and tanks in the garden courtyard included a rectangular pool approximately 13.80 by 6.80 metres of around AD 275–300. Fed from a fine Hamstone culvert block, it was possibly a fish pool. The four tanks were also employed as garden features; one has been claimed as a nymphaeum. A fragmentary sculpted scallop in Hamstone hints at a fountain feature. At the late third-century Bancroft villa, a fish pool some 13 by 2.6 metres enhanced the axial view from the villa's central reception room. At Gadebridge Park the 21.75 by 13 metre natatio replaced a smaller, early fourth-century one measuring approximately 11.60 by 6.30 metres. In the late Antonine era, Gadebridge also had a rectangular water basin measuring 5.48 by 4.11 metres constructed in front of the villa axial to the central room. Recent ground-penetrating radar work at Keynsham's Roman 'villa' suggests a rectangular pool around 11 by 4 metres sits

The huge complex at Darenth, Kent, is one of Britain's most intriguing. It featured an impressive pool visually leading to a nymphaeum and a temple shrine. Walled market gardens and orchards surrounded the inner garden.

in the centre of the courtyard. Another rectangular pool 11.9 by 4.5 metres was found at Well in Yorkshire. It was 1.8 metres in depth and stood alone, perhaps in a garden in front of an ill-understood complex. The existence of a double-S cresting block in the pool's infill, as also ornamented the nymphaeum at Chedworth, suggests it was a sacred pool. Enigmatic circular marks on the bottom stones of the pool, in front of the aqueduct inlet, perhaps suggest a bronze pool sculpture.

A remarkable British pool is that from Darenth, Kent, measuring 25.6 by 3.3 metres and running north–south at a slight angle from the centre of the Roman complex within a walled garden enclosure. Retained by massive tiled walls, the metre-deep pool yielded elaborate wall plaster. From the north-east corner came a little bronze lioness or panther head spout, probably once fixed to a cantharus fountain as is postulated for North Leigh. The view from the building's central room stretched down to the end of the canal where it ended in a semicircular nymphaeum pool. This was 0.42 metres deep, 1.46 metres wide at the centre and with a rear wall 2.89 metres long that was retained by massive piers and probably rose higher than the bowed front. Whether its waters overflowed into the main pool is unknown, but the remains of a 0.22-metre-wide inlet survived at the back east corner and a broken outlet at the west. The structure backing the nymphaeum pool spectacularly framed the view of a 4.96-metre-square vaulted building, with an ornamental porch 10.6 metres to the south that was almost certainly a temple. Darenth has always seemed to the author to have more of a public feel rather than that of a private villa. Countering its size, wealth, considerable bathing facilities and gardens is the surprising lack of mosaics and domestic refinements evident. Perhaps one should see here a water shrine and hostelry, similar to that postulated for Great Witcombe and Chedworth.

A new reconstruction of the state complex at Cannon Street, London, based on excavation reports. The pool is the most elaborate known from Britannia. (Author)

Apart from Caerleon's natatio at the legionary baths it boasted two more long rectangular open-air pools with apsidal ends. The 'hippodrome garden' of the praetorium had a 90-cm-deep example, while the 'Castle Baths' had another apsidal natatio in its palaestra.

The most elaborate British pool is that in the garden of the Thameside complex once known as 'the Governor's Palace' in London and valiantly recorded and excavated by Peter Marsden during destructive redevelopment between 1961 and 1972. Excavations in 1988–89 disproved the palace's projected west wing and its attachment to buildings to its east and south. Grand and official, it was the location of the London stone – perhaps Britannia's golden milestone. The pool was 10.06 metres wide by over 30.48 metres long and around 1.83 metres deep, with two minor pools on the north side. Bases in these pools probably held fountains or statues, and a later foundation at the east end again may have held a fountain. On the south side was an angular recess that seems likely to have been matched on the north. The garden terrace itself was formed by thick dumps of clay and gravel, but the surface was destroyed by bulldozers without any excavation being permitted. The author's reconstruction takes a new interpretation from excavation reports. Allied to the London pool's design, Wroxeter's baths had an elegant example in its palaestra or garden with 'shouldered apses' at each end resembling the design used at the Villa of the Papyri, Herculaneum.

Several villas in the south-west of England with copious springs in their vicinity are likely to have had pools that have not yet been traced. At Box and Castle Copse villas, modern ponds are centred over part of the courtyard garden at the former and on the central axis of the Roman building at the latter. Great Witcombe, Woodchester and Chedworth all hold great prospects for water features. At the latter site a spout emptying water from the central court into a stone tank leading to the lower court was uncovered in 2018.

CHAPTER 9

Piscinae and Natationes

The keeping and breeding of fish for food, pleasure and aesthetics was greatly desired and many garden piscinae (fishponds) give hints that they were once inhabited. The most obvious is the presence of pots or amphorae imbedded in the pond's walls to form retreats for breeding or shade. Sometimes the pond is very small, such as in the House of Gavius Rufus at Pompeii. That measured 2.17 by 1.06 metres, but others were monumental, such as on the Palatine or the great cross-shaped pool of the Herculaneum palaestra with its five-headed serpent fountain. Not all pools had breeding holes and it is believed that rhythmically niched borders also provided shelter and shade for fish. The pond could be shaded by a pergola as in the House of the Centenary, Pompeii. Fishponds required circulation of water and a minimum depth of 50 cm to be successful and, with the construction of aqueducts, their presence in city gardens proliferated. The ponds outside the triclinia at Conimbriga's two grandest houses remind one of Martial's friend who, from his couch, fished for his dinner in the pool below the triclinium window of his seaside villa at Formia (Martial, *Epigrams X*, 16–21).

In the early years of the empire freshwater fishponds were considered plebeian and inferior to those at the wealthy seaside villas. The spectacular fishponds attached to villae maritimae were greatly desired and have left astonishing remains. Eating sea fish from such pools was a status symbol and one fish might equal a skilled labourer's daily wage. At Torre Astura a maritime villa was attached by a 130-metre bridge to an amazing sea-bound artificial island featuring dozens of geometrically designed tanks girded by a seawall 172 by 175 metres. A central terrace held maritime pleasure chambers. So substantial are these sea-girt remains that they formed the base on which the sets for Alexandria and Cleopatra's palace were erected for the 1963 epic *Cleopatra*. Men attending to fishponds at such a maritime villa appear on a mosaic from Aquilea now in the Venice Archaeological Museum.

Maritime fishponds were particularly frequent around the Bay of Naples. The Sorrento villa of Agrippa Postumus was built on terraces above and below the cliffs now occupied by the hotel Bellevue Syrene. It featured sea-girt fishponds, baths, nymphaea and grottoes in the cliff with rock-cut tanks and circulation channels. At Sperlonga the Grotto of Tiberius preserves fishponds linked to the sea. A rectangular pond surrounds an island enclosing four tanks and a triclinum platform fronting the circular pool within the grotto. A second grotto pool adjoins to the north-east. The island is thickly peppered with fish refuges and freshwater springs top up the pools and turn the water brackish. Marine fishponds require the waters to be renewed and profit from an intake of spring water. Beyond the ponds the outer area flooded at high tide and was overlooked by a dining pavilion and portico that predated the central island.

In Britain, considering the craze for fishponds among Roman aristocrats and its proximity to the sea, the villa maritima at Fishbourne should have been equipped with one. The known pond in the southern garden may well have held freshwater fish. It was 9 metres across, but

Part of the huge fish farm attached to a great villa maritima at Torre Astura on the Bay of Antium. The medieval tower covers some of the villa buildings.

its original form is unknown. North of it a larger pool is thought to have extended along the south side of the baths. A base for a statue or urn stood beside it to the west. It would be odd for a saltwater fishpool not to be attempted and one wonders if the known 'deep water channel' discovered fronting the southern terrace might possibly be interpreted as one especially as a stretch of the necessary freshwater pipeline for topping-up standing seawater was found leading towards it.

Bancroft villa's fourth-century pool included breeding holes. The presence of fish should certainly be expected in pools such as Eccles, Darenth, Halstock or any connected to a water source. At Ivy Chimneys, Essex, the third-century-AD Romano-Celtic temple overlooked a large rectangular 18-by-22-metre pond that contained the remains of freshwater fish. The pond had a cobbled base and a sophisticated water regulation system. Fish were farmed at Shakenoak villa in Oxfordshire between AD 70 and AD 200, with the water of its three ponds retained by oak timbers. The water flow connecting the small breeding pool, the main pool and the holding pool was controlled by oak valves that survived. It is also postulated for Claydon Pike in Gloucestershire. The recent discovery of fish bones in a corn drier at Doynton Villa in South Gloucestershire suggests some level of fish farming and the smoking of fish on that estate. A third-century, 13-by-35-metre stone-lined pond at Lynch Farm, Peterborough, was first believed to be a fishpond. A later idea saw it for salt production as the Nene was tidal at this point, but possibly it was for sea fish.

It may seem strange to modern sensibilities, but swimming pools (natationes) like Gadebridge's or the 30-by-3-metre rectangular pool in Herculaneum's great palaestra also occasionally had breeding holes for fish, suggesting that just as amorini swim with fish on mosaics so could those using pools. After all, natural watercourses and the sea had fish. The open air natatio at the 'Fortress Baths' (Caerleon) dated to around AD 100–110 and measured

A huge villa maritima with a walled, heavily wooded garden and a fish farm on a mosaic from Aquilea in Venice Archaeological Museum. The inner peristyle is grassed.

an impressive 41 by 6.4 metres. Huge swimming pools were a feature of gardens at Cherchell, Oplontis A, Villa dei Centroni (Colli Albani) and the Villa San Marco at Stabiae. Several, such as that in the 'Building with the Fishpond' or the huge pool at the Pecile, were features of Hadrian's Tivoli villa.

Herod's Promontory Palace at Caesarea included a rock-cut pool measuring 18 by 35 metres. It was surrounded by colonnades with intercolumnar rock-cut pits for shrubs and trees. At Herodium a huge 70 by 45 metre garden pool had a central tholos and swimming pools also existed at his palaces at Masada and at Jericho, where that at the third palace measured 90 by 42 metres. In Petra a large garden and pool complex was built for Aretus IV, perhaps in imitation of Herod's.

Paestum has two unusual pools that may have stood within gardens and been both piscinae and natationes. Dating to the third century BC, the Pool of Fortuna Virilis measures 47 by 21 metres and has a rectangular island raised on stone piers, like a hypocaust. Possibly the scene of sacred ceremonies connected to Venus and the Veneralia or swimming competitions. The

The great marble swimming pool at Oplontis A, fronting the east wing. Originally a series of statues and herms were spaced along the left-hand bank, each fronting a tree in the fashionable way.

Herod the Great's palace at Caesarea Maritima featured a central swimming pool surrounded by colonnades and rock-cut bedding trenches. (Courtesy of Mike Stone)

A rare photograph of the 1890s of the huge and little-known pools at Cherchell (anciently Caesarea Mauretaniae) on the coast of Algeria. (Author's collection)

The Nymphaeum of Thubursicum Numidarum with its swimming pools and shrines. (Courtesy of Marigold Norbye)

The sacred swimming pool at Heliopolis (Hammam Beda) was probably connected to a temple garden. (Courtesy of Marigold Norbye)

island's shade would also have sheltered fish. The second pool at the House of the Swimming Pool dates to the early imperial period and again includes a stage-like area covering the water at one end.

Cherchell, Algeria, had a spectacular isolated 36-by-10-metres harbour-side pool, possibly set in a temple or bath's garden. At either end square statue pedestals were joined to the poolside by arches that perhaps once held water pipes for fountains. In the centre was a massive base, perhaps for a Scylla group. Deep steps were later inserted at the pool's corners. An additional C-shaped nymphaeum pool adjoined the rectangular basin at its western side. As at Darenth, its walls appear the same height as those of the great pool, so whether their waters connected is unknown. The Algerian Nymphaeum of Thubursicum Numidarum (Khemissa) consists of two adjoining basins with brackish waters. The first rectangular pool, with a depth of 1.40 metres, is 47 by 13 metres, while the other starts rectangular, 18.50 metres wide, but ends in horseshoe, 26.50 metres in diameter. Both were used for swimming. Shrines bordered the first pool on the south where remains of a huge statue of Diana were found, while a temple, possibly to Neptune, and fronted by a portico garden occupied the north. Between the basins a narrow canal carried drinking water from Aïn-el-Bir, 400 metres away, and overflowed into the second basin. The pools were reputedly the source of the River Medjerda, which irrigates northern Tunisia. Also in Algeria is the sacred circular Roman natatio of Heliopolis (Hammam Berda), which is believed to have been set in a temple garden or precinct. Its basin is 36 metres in diameter and filled at a projecting hemicycle by a spring with a temperature of 29.3 °C and tempered by a cold water spring.

CHAPTER 10

Public Gardens

Baths

Although Rome's imperial baths had gardens for health and relaxation, the evidence for them elsewhere is archaeologically lacking. Even Conimbriga's has recently been questioned. They might be expected at some of the huge provincial establishments, but even in places like Carthage or Trier evidence is absent. Plantings may have fringed outdoor natationes, as a stolen mosaic from Apamea showing a garden surrounding a bath building depicts. A bronze Hercules statue stands by a waterwheel. An inscription from Salamis (Cyprus) dedicates a new (but unlocated) garden. Excavations in Sparta have, however, discovered a public garden south-east

A unique representation of bathers in an outdoor natatio connected to a bath complex. The baths are set in a garden and plants fringe the pool. The mosaic depicting the foundation of Apamea was stolen and is only known from this photograph issued by Interpol and taken on a mobile phone.

The great palaestra or campus at Pompeii was surrounded by a shading double row of plane trees whose root casts remain. These have now been replanted. (Courtesy of Marigold Norbye)

of the baths in Triakosion Street. It was walled with towers bearing spouts that filled small quatrefoil basins. These overflowed into a flanking euripus. The great pool at Cherchell may also indicate another garden attached to baths. Pompeii and Herculaneum's great palaestrae were bordered with shading trees and the same idea might be expected at other such campi as Caerleon's. Baths were placed to afford bathers fine views of landscape or gardens from their large caldarium windows.

Theatre Gardens

Where possible, Roman theatres were provided with gardens. These were often attached to the porticus post scaenam, and located behind the theatre's stage building the scaenae frons. Here audiences gathered during intermissions, took refreshment or sheltered from storms. They were also used for chorus rehearsals. Generally the attached garden consisted of a large open courtyard laid to lawns or shrubberies and surrounded by a quadriporticus. Public promenades divided these gardens. Vitruvius' *On Architecture*, Book V, chapter 9, remarks how healthy these hypaethral walks were for citizens. The presence of plants improved eyesight, walking diminished corpulency, and promenading in gardens carried off noxious humours from their bodies. He wrote, 'there can be no doubt of the necessity of making spacious and pleasant walks open to the air in every city.'

It was expected that the promenades themselves would be properly drained to avoid mud. Vitruvius advised laying drains and founding the paths on coals with a levelled gravel topping.

The garden of the Pompeian theatre quadriporticus as replanted by Giuseppe Spano in the early years of the last century. (Author's collection)

The restored theatre quadriporticus of the theatre at Merida gives a good idea of the pleasures of such foundations.

The most famous theatre garden was Rome's Porticus of Pompey, the Ambulatio Magni, which opened in 62 BC at the rear of Pompey's theatre. While the piazza ambulatories were lined with rows of plane trees and two euripi, the porticos were a gallery of the artworks liberated during Pompey's campaigns. Its magnificence led to emulation throughout the empire. Following the AD 62 earthquake, Pompeii's first-century-BC quadriporticus became the gladiators' barracks. Around 1920 Giuseppe Spano, Pompeii's director of excavations, influenced by the Ambulatio Magni, had its garden replanted with two great rectangular beds filled with olive and plane trees surrounded by box hedging. It survives only in photographs. The restored theatre garden at Mérida gives a splendid idea of how refreshing a quadriporticus might have appeared. Surrounded by a water channel, the niched rectangular flower beds of 'the island' resemble those of a water garden. A shrine to the imperial cult was a feature of that quadriporticus. At Italica the garden was surrounded by a monumental double Tuscan portico and included a central niched euripus canal, a water tank and a temple of Isis built into the western portico.

Portico Gardens

Allied to theatre and temple gardens were the formal public spaces or porticos such as Augustus' magnificent Porticus Liviae in Rome, which contained garden walks, exedrae, fountains and artworks. One of the vines that shaded its ambulatories produced twelve amphorae of wine per annum. Such porticos were imitated elsewhere. Related were Pompeii's Eumachia building and Vaison-la-Romaine's so-called 'portico sanctuary', whose gardens included a large central fishpond and an island perhaps holding a shrine. Similarly, at Nimes, porticos and gardens surrounded the waters of the Augusteum. At Italica a small triangular park lay just within the north gate. The popularity of such portico parks for promenading and relaxation encouraged their addition to other public buildings such as temples, baths and libraries. Ovid considered the Porticus Liviae, and the Ambulatio Magni good places to pick up women (*Ars Amatoria*, Books 1 and 3).

The portico sanctuary at Vaison-la-Romaine. A quadriporticus surrounded a garden with a large pool with an apsidal end seen here. On the right part of the central island that held a temple may be seen.

Temple Gardens

It is likely that many Roman temples had plantings in their precincts. The Greek sacred grove or alsos was a median place between two worlds, where man met divinities through nature – hence green trees constantly watered by a spring in an otherwise arid landscape was a wonder and caused by a divine presence. Temple gardens developed from sacred groves. Sappho's sixth-century hymn to Aphrodite ('Sappho 2') sings of a temple surrounded by an apple orchard with a spring and ground cover of roses.

Athens' Temple of Hephaistos had a garden in the third century BC that lasted until at least the age of Nero. Rock-cut pits in rows held trees and shrubs on three sides of the temple in this Garden of Hephaistos containing such plants as pomegranates, myrtle, vines, ivy and bay. The temenos of Didyma's colossal Temple of Apollo in Turkey had an extensive grove on its western side. In the third century BC, the vast open-air adyton had a sacred spring and a grove of bay trees planted before the naiskos. Their leaves were used for garlands and mantic rituals. The terraced temenos of Diana at Nemi held an ancient grove where Aeneas had plucked the Golden Bough.

Excavations of temple precincts often show that plantings are spaced, linear and formal. A spaced row of planting pits, perhaps for bay trees, flanked the podium of Pompeii's Temple of Apollo. Pompeii's Temple of Venus had alternating deep and shallow pits flanking the gutters of the surrounding portico, suggesting that their plantings alternated in height. Perhaps roses and myrtle bushes grew here. This regularity was not followed at Pompeii's triclinia-fronted Temple of Dionysos, where informally planted trees and a vine arbour shaded diners while a vineyard backed it. At Empúries, Spain, the Capitolium was flanked by hanging rectangular garden beds. Munigua's Temple of the Podium atop the terraced sanctuary was flanked by two small rectangular pools and geometrically spaced 'sacred groves'. Likewise, a garden surrounded Mérida's Temple of Diana, while two rectangular pools with statuary and fountains flanked it. Occasionally pools alone enlivened a temenos. The podium of the Temple of Diana at Evora, Portugal, was surrounded by a U-shaped pool. At Timgad, Algeria, the miraculous spring Aqua Septimiana Felix that gave life to the town was aggrandised in AD 213. Three temples overlooked a courtyard more than 150 by 44 metres, forming the largest religious building in Roman Africa. The complex was probably a healing centre dedicated to the waters and the Imperial cult. A pool 27 by 7 metres, surrounded by a bronze balustrade and filled by the spring, stood before the central temple and on axis with it and the great square with its painted porticos. With so much water one might expect formal plantings. At El Jem the Temple of the Imperial Cult had porticoes and rooms paved with a water-pattern mosaic and a huge courtyard with two long parallel pools.

The Temple of Juno at Gabii near Rome was surrounded by thirty-four spaced planting pits. In Rome, the Temple of the Divine Claudius (restored by Vespasian) had fountains fed by the Aqua Claudia and was surrounded by multiple linear planting beds. Vespasian's Temple of Peace, celebrating the Jewish campaign, was inaugurated in AD 75. Its piazza was only paved along the northern entrance side. The rest was floored with beaten earth or grass reduced to that state. It was a water garden with two groups of three fountains flanking the central area of the piazza facing the main temple façade. These fountains consisted of long, rectangular marble-clad platforms over which ran a constant light-catching film of water. Gutters surrounded them and hedges of Gallica roses were planted alongside. At the Palatine's Vigna Barberini, Elagabulus' colossal Heliogabalium was flanked by a formal garden of long narrow beds and numerous planting pits.

Temple gardens and plantings did not have to be extensive. The reconstruction of the Chichester Jupiter column imagines a temenos in Noviomagus. Evidence for sacred plantings in Britain and the Northern Provinces is mostly circumstantial. Sacred trees and groves are well attested in Celtic religion and suspected at such sites as Gosbecks Farm, Colchester, and where eccentrically placed temples within a temenos suggest that they stood beside one. At Ivy Chimneys, Essex, the temple overlooked a fishpond, presumably part of a garden setting.

The so-called 'Temple of Diana' at Merida was flanked by pools and fountains within a garden.

The long marble fountains of Vespasian's Temple of Peace as excavated. The fountains were flanked by beds of Gallica roses. The paved entrance court of the garden appears beyond.

The Heliogabalium on the Palatine and its garden made for the exhibition 'Il Giardino dei Cesari' at the Terme Museum, Rome, in 2001.

A temple precinct garden in Noviomagus Reginorum showing the Chichester Jupiter column restored. (Author)

Aftermath

Gardens survive as long as people find benefit in their existence. They were part of 'Romanitas'. The Western Empire's collapse in the fifth century AD must have affected their survival, but would hardly have destroyed them all. Many must have become market gardens, especially considering the famines, plagues and interruption in trade that occurred. The Christian Church preserved elements in its cloisters and monastery gardens. In the Eastern Empire they certainly survived, and water gardens in particular would influence the Muslim invaders of the seventh century, who eventually reintroduced them into Spain. The water gardens of Granada's Alhambra Palace are in essence the imitators of ancient Rome's.

The water gardens of the Alhambra are the descendants of those of ancient Rome.

Further Reading

Adembri, Benedetta, *Hadrian's Villa* (Milan, 2014)

Almon, Clopper, *Exploring Roman Gardens in Spain and Portugal* (London, 2016)

Andreae, Bernard and Claudio Presicce, *Ulisse: Il Mito e la Memoria* (Sperlonga: Rome, 1996)

Bezin, Christine et al., *Vaison la Romaine: Antique Médiévale et Moderne* (Vaison, 2006)

Bowe, Patrick, *Gardens of the Roman World* (London, 2004)

Campanelli, Adele, *Rosantico: Natura, Bellezza, Gusto, Profumi tra Paestum, Padula e Velia* (Paestum, 2013)

Carey, Sorcha, *Pliny's Catalogue of Culture* (Oxford, 2003)

Carroll, Maureen, *Earthly Paradises: Ancient Gardens in History and Archaeology* (London, 2003)

Ciarallo, Annamaria, *Orti e Giardini di Pompei* (Naples, 1992)

Ciarallo, Annamaria, *Gardens of Pompeii* (Rome, 2000)

Cima, Maddalena and Eugenio La Rocca, *Le Tranquille Dimore Degli Dei. La Residenza Imperial Degli Horti Lamiani* (Vicenza, 1986)

Correia, Virgilio, *Conimbriga: Guide to the Ruins* (Lisbon, 2017)

Cunliffe, Barry, *Excavations at Fishbourne*, Vols I and II (London, 1971)

Cunliffe, Barry et al, *Chichester Excavations IX: Excavations at Fishbourne: 1969–1988* (Chichester, 1996)

Farrer, Linda, *Ancient Roman Gardens* (Stroud, 1998)

Featherstone, Michael et al. (ed), *The Emperor's House: Palaces from Augustus to the Age of Absolutism* (Berlin/Boston, 2015)

Gazda, Elaine and John Clarke (eds), *Leisure and Luxury in the Age of Nero: The Villas of Oplontis Near Pompeii* (Ann Arbor, 2016)

Higginbotham, James, *Piscinae: Artificial Fishponds in Roman Italy* (Chapel Hill and London, 1997)

Hoffmann, Adolf and Ulrike Wulf, *Die Kaiserpaläste auf dem Palatin in Rom* (Mainz, 2006)

Jashemski, Wilhelmina, *The Gardens of Pompeii, Herculaneum and the Villas Destroyed by Vesuvius* (New York, 1979)

Jashemski, Wilhelmina, *The Gardens of Pompeii, Herculaneum and the Villas Destroyed by Vesuvius. Volume II: Appendices* (New York, 1993)

Jashemski, Wilhelmina et al, *Gardens of the Roman Empire* (Cambridge, 2017)

Jashemski, Wilhelmina and Frederick Meyer, *Natural History of Pompeii* (Cambridge, 2002)

Lanciani, Rodolfo, *The Ruins and Excavations of Ancient Rome* (London, 1897)

MacDonald, William, *Hadrian's Villa and Its Legacy* (New Haven and London, 1995)

MacDougall, Elisabeth et al, *Ancient Roman Gardens* (Washington, 1981)

MacDougall, Elisabeth (ed.), *Ancient Roman Villa Gardens* (Washington, 1987)

Manley, John and David Rudkin, *Facing the Palace: Excavations in Front of the Roman Palace at Fishbourne, 1995–1999* (Lewes, 2003)

Marzano, Annalisa and Guy Metraux (eds.), *The Roman Villa in the Mediterranean Basin: Late Republic to Late Antiquity* (Cambridge, 2018)

Mattusch, Carol, *Pompeii and the Roman Villa: Art and Culture around the Bay of Naples* (London, 2008)

Mayer, Lavinia (ed.), *AquaRomana: Human Technique and Divine Force* (Barcelona, 2004)

Mielsch, Harald, *Die Römische Villa: Architektur und Lebensform* (Munich, 1987)

Morvillez, Eric and Clopper Almon, *Exploring Roman Gardens In and Near France* (London, 2016)

Netzer, Ehud, *The Architecture of Herod the Great Builder* (Grand Rapids, 2008)

Pesce, Angelo, *Otium Ludens: Leisure and Play: Ancient Relics of the Roman Empire* (Hong Kong, 2008)

Pessoa, Miguel and Lino Rodrigo, *Museum. Catalogue; Roman Villa of Rabacal* (Penela, 2005)

Prisset, Jean-Luc, *Guide de Site: Saint-Romain-en-Gal* (Paris, 1999)

Rozenberg, Silvia and David Mevorah (eds), *Herod the Great: The King's Final Journey* (Jerusalem, 2013)

Ryley, Claire, *Roman Gardens and Their Plants* (Lewes, 1998)

Sabrié, Raymond and Maryse Sabrié, *Roman Narbonne: The Clos de la Lombarde, an ancient quarter* (Narbonne, 2015)

Settis, Salvatore, *La Pareti Ingannevoli: La Villa di Livia a la Pittura di Giardino* (Milan, 2006)

Sojc, Natascha, *Domus Augustana* (Leiden, 2012)

Stefani, Grete (ed.) *Man and the Environment in the Territory of Vesuvius: The Antiquarium of Boscoreale* (Pompeii, 2010)

Thompson, Dorothy Burr and Ralph Griswold, *Garden Lore of Ancient Athens* (Princeton, 1963)

Villedieu, Francoise, *Il Giardino dei Cesari: Dai Palazzi antichi alla Vigna Barberini sul Monte Palatino* (Rome, 2001)

The destruction of Bignor villa as imagined by Alan Sorrell. In foot, the villa shows no signs of having been sacked but gradually decayed. (Courtesy and copyright of Julia Sorrell)